Genealogical How-to Letters

"When Your Ox is in the Ditch"

by

Vera McDowell

GENEALOGICAL PUBLISHING Co. Inc.

W9-BMH-579

Southern Echoes

Monograph Series
Special Publication Number One

Originally published by the
Augusta Genealogical Society, Inc.
Augusta, Georgia

Reprinted 1995 by the
Genealogical Publishing Co., Inc.
1001 N. Calvert St., Baltimore, Md. 21202
Second printing 1996
Third printing 1997

Library of Congress Catalogue Card Number 95-78281
International Standard Book Number 0-8063-1484-2
Made in the United States of America

Table of Contents

Publisher's Acknowledgments

The Augusta Genealogical Society, Inc. is indebted to the following members for their contributions toward making possible Special Publications Number One in the Society's Southern Echoes Monograph Series. It is through their collective talents and immense generosity that this compilation of letters comes into the hands of genealogists, to help them bypass those inevitable potholes in the research road.

VERA M. McDOWELL, author of the letters in this compilation. Vera's letters are often on subjects not addressed in standard genealogical methodology primers; her observations about common-sense approaches to daily research problems are full of practical wisdom and self-effacing humor. Her sustained contribution to the genealogical community is a far-reaching one, and to the members of this Society, a continuing one.

HARRY T. EVANS, illustrator. Harry's humorous art is a perfect extension of Vera's sense of humor. His light-hearted drawings introducing the chapters are treasures, and sure to bring chuckles from others who have followed the same research road. Harry holds awards from juried exhibitions for his serious art.

WILIAM T. (Troup) MORTON, Sr., illustrator. Troup's art on pages 45 and 97 supplements Harry's drawings and adds much to the "feel" of the subjects. As an attorney, Troup well knows Georgia courthouses and as a Jones County, Georgia, native, is surely familiar with old homesteads.

CARRIE M. ADAMSON, editor. Long-time editor of Vera's monthly letters in <u>Southern Echoes</u>, Carrie arranged the collection into chapters for this publication, while indulging an editorial sense of humor as she wrote titles and introductions for the chapters and letters. The book's design, layout, and camera-ready copy are hers.

Dr. WILLIAM G. BILTON, associate editor. A marvel of modern technology helped "Bill" bring his editorial talents to bear on the typing for publication of these letters. Setting up attractive titles and joining in editorial judgments were further appreciated contributions. His mother, Peggy, was also involved in the final production.

LaVIECE SMALLWOOD, columnist, author. LaViece initiated the idea of publishing Vera's letters in book form, and has been a firm supporter of the efforts to do so.

RUSSELL R. MOORES, Society president. His support of this project from its inception contributed greatly to its completion.

Foreword

As anyone new to genealogical research soon learns, there's more to the study of family history than merely finding names and dates to tack to a family tree. It's a whole other world waiting out there in research land, waiting to dazzle your senses, excite your emotions, and challenge your intellect.

It's a world where the search never ends, where the researcher remains alert to find what his ancestor did, ate, wore, voted for, shot at, and dreamed about. Where he lived, and the spirit of adventure that pushed him ever onward to seek new land and new frontiers. How he fought wars and cleared fields. What his triumphs--and his sorrows--were and how his religion shaped his life. How he fell in love with and married the neighbor's daughter, built his home, paid his taxes, raised a family, helped his neighbor. And coped. In short, family research is a big Detective Game.

And that's what these compiled letters by Vera McDowell are all about. Never mind the deepest potholes along the research road, she says, there's a way around them. Instead, enjoy smelling the roses you find along the way. In a word, she offers help with problem-solving, so one can spend more time having fun making discoveries. In fact, she makes a good case for doing genealogy at all: for the FUN of it. She notes that the world of adventure she knows so much about can offer frustration, bewilderment, or disappointment, as well as satisfaction, joy, fulfillment, and pure pleasure. She sees her role as eliminating the first and accentuating the second category.

The first of Vera's letters appeared in the Augusta Genealogical Society's monthly newsletter, <u>Southern</u> <u>Echoes</u>, in July, 1982; the series continues. Her common-sense, practical advice soon gained the author a wide following, and her mailbox has a steady flow of letters from individuals seeking advice, making her somewhat of a "Dear Abby" in genealogical circles.

As a researcher, Vera has "been there," having traced her own families back to early New England, with one line to Sandwich, Massachusetts in 1635. She served four years as Registrar of the Augusta Chapter, DAR, and is currently Registrar of the Reverend Pierre Robert Chapter, Colonial Dames of the XVII Century.

As a columnist, she is an editor's delight, with an enormous sense of humor, a mind open to suggestions, and a grasp of the knotty problems a researcher faces--problems that all too often have answers which no one ever bothers to pass on. The need for documenting and organizational detail, a knowledge of historical background, quips on the searcher's world as she sees it, changes in research patterns brought about by modern technology--these and more are the subjects she addresses with humor and gusto.

The title, <u>When</u> <u>Your</u> <u>Ox</u> <u>is</u> <u>in</u> <u>the</u> <u>Ditch</u>, has its roots in the Bible (Luke 14:5). It is an old expression often used in the South to convey a thought common to anyone who has ever gone down the research road: a condition where one is in dire need of help from someone, anyone, to move things forward! Vera's letters answer that call.

It is the hope of the Society that these letters will be as useful to present and future genealogists as they have been to Vera's fans in the past.

Carrie Adamson, Editor
13 August 1992

Dedicated to

My husband, James M. McDowell, for the best 45 years of my life.

My cousin, Bette Kahler, and her husband Charles, who were always
       there when I needed them the most.

My grandfather, William J. Marshall, for instilling in me the love of
       family research and the need to know "from whence I came."

My brothers, Richard, Kenneth, William, and Bertrum Marshall,
       who, each in his own way, contributed to the person
       I am today.

My best friends, Carrie Adamson and Barbara Rhoades, for
       all the years they have shared with me their thoughts, their love,
       and many hours of laughter.

The Augusta Genealogical Society, for allowing me to have so darn
       much fun during the years they have published my articles.

Vera M. McDowell (1992)

Chapter 1

Getting the Record Straight

Order--or Chaos? All depends on getting your notes and files organized. Don't, and it's Chaos! Keep your files simple and open-ended, and for Heaven's sake, document as you go along--<u>that's</u> Order.

CHECK AND DOUBLE CHECK. Some of us, in our excitement over finding a family line, are prone to accept another's documentation. If you do, you may be in for some surprises when the truth comes out!

{V}

Augusta, Georgia

Dear Bette,

It's impossible! You're too new at this game to have already proven a line back to the 1600s. Besides, I did this line years ago--it's not ours and I can prove it; will send you the correct material. In the meantime, go back to that family history and check the dates again (They did marry young in those days, but it's still hard to believe a man became a father when he was nine years old!). You've learned a valuable lesson--don't accept someone else's information! Obviously you need some basic guidelines, so let me tell you a few rules that I follow with every new line.

First, always "start at the end," which is yourself, and work back from there.

Second, document as you go. Get a photocopy as soon as you've found a record; you may not get back that way again. Send for a copy of your birth record, this will give your parents' ages and birthplaces, and your mother's maiden name. You already know this? Don't count on it! I searched every town in Connecticut for Daddy's birth only to learn later that he was born in Maine. So, don't ever assume that you know anything; search it out and prove it.

A word of caution on these documents: everything there is not always the truth. For instance, on a death record the doctor listed his patient's name and date, cause, and place of death. This much you know is factual; question all other data, as it's only as good as the informant's knowledge of the deceased. On one of mine, the son of the deceased said his grandmother was Matilda Wall when she actually was Sultana Wall (I should have stuck with Matilda!). Get the idea?

Third, when you've found your ancestor in the Town Records, don't stop there. Copy ALL the children of his parents. I know, you're only after him, but sometimes it's the only way to get a general idea of when his parents were married, such as, the first child was born 1798, they married sometime prior to that? There are other advantages too, which I'll explain next.

Fourth, SAVE EVERYTHING!! You'll collect loads of stuff along the way, all pertaining to your family surname, which you're sure doesn't belong to YOUR family. Don't be too sure. Write each surname on a file folder and put all these tidbits in it for safe-keeping. Mine are filed that way in file boxes marked "The Morgue" (I KNEW you'd love that!). I had three of these boxes, covering a 15-year search for the parents of my William Marshall, and when they were finally found, I was able to put together three generations of their family, all proved and documented.

Well, dear, that's it for tonight. Think about what you want to ask and let me know. But, PLEASE, no more questions right now about dates; go for something else, something easy. Okay?

Love,

Vera

CITE YOUR SOURCES. Why keeping a record of where information is found is important to the genealogist: It prevents tedious researching.

$\boxed{V}$

Augusta, Georgia

Dear Bette,

In going through my letters to you I find that I've overlooked one important phase of your "education," the need to keep a record of "where you search for what." If you don't keep a record, then you'll waste time and money going over the same stuff over and over again. Special charts are available for this purpose, but you can make your own, using a loose-leaf notebook with lined paper, and drawing the vertical lines for your columns. Use a separate notebook for each state and mark the name on the spine for easy identification. Inside, you put subject dividers with all the surnames being searched in that state printed on the tabs. It's just like setting up office files, only more fun. There comes a time in your search when you know an ancestor was born somewhere else, and not in the town where you found him as an adult. The search begins, to find where he did come from. A portion of one of my charts follows, with an explanation.

I found John Wheeler in the History of Boothbay, Maine and it said..."he came here from the northeastern part of Mass.," that several sons served in the Rev. War, that he married Judith Knight in 1769, and that he was age 67 when he died in 1777. From this I got a search area, a probable birth year, and the fact that Judith was not his first wife, since her sons would have been too young for military service in 1776. I chose to search Essex County, Massachusetts first, as most of the early settlers of Maine came from towns in that county, and the Essex County History showed Wheelers in the towns on my chart.

Vera M. McDowell 2307 Harding Rd. Augusta, GA 30906 23 Sept 1971	Name...........John WHEELER, b. ca. 1710 Search Area......Essex Co., Mass. No records = O Found records = X		
Sources Searched	Gloucester	Salisbury	Rowley
History of Essex Co.	X	O	X
Town History of	X	O	X
Vital Records of	X	O	X

What was found is listed on the bottom of the chart as so:
In Rowley...John Wheeler, b. 10 March 1710, s/o David and Hannah; his marriage in 1730 to the widow Abigail Brown; and the birth of their daughter Abigail, 20 May 1732

In Gloucester...died 1734, Abigail, wife of John Wheeler; the marriage of John to Ann Sargent, 3 Dec. 1735; birth of seven children, 1737 to 1754; and the death of Ann, wife of John Wheeler, in 1767

In the History of Gloucester, Massachusetts...John Wheeler, after the death of his wife, took his children and moved to Kennebec River area of Maine.

So, right on one chart you have everything--<u>who</u> you looked for, <u>where</u> you looked, <u>what</u> you found, and <u>when</u> they were there (back to the four "W's" again!). And if you're smart, you'll make photocopies of the records <u>when</u> you find them!

That's all for now. If you have any questions you know where <u>I</u> am (at least).

Love,
Vera

SEE-THROUGHS & POST-ITS--DANDY & HANDY!! Old letters or documents are visible and easy to handle in those dandy, new top-loaders. And as for handy Post-Its, their uses are limited only by your imagination, ingenuity, and clever ideas!

{v}

Augusta, Georgia

Dear Bette,

It was good to hear from you again, and I was as thrilled as you to hear that you'd found a box of old letters. Your question as to how to preserve them gave me the idea for this letter. To start with--do not punch holes in them!! There's a much better way. Have you ever gone shopping at the school supply department of your local discount store? Try it, you'll love it!! They have all kinds of aids for the researchers, not just pens, pencils, and notebooks.

For a starter, they have top-loading 8-1/2x11 poly sheet protectors. Never seen them? We all use scads of them! They allow you to slide a paper, document, photograph, etc. into the top and know that it won't slide out, as it's sealed on three sides. They have a reinforced binding edge with three holes punched in it so you can put them in a notebook (without having to punch holes into precious documents). They are clear, so that you can read everything through them, and you can photocopy whatever is in them without removing it from its protective cover. And most are archival-safe, which means that the cover won't damage whatever you've placed inside. The top-loaders come in many sizes, making it convenient for us to use them for any number of things.

Another useful item is a see-through refill for a photograph album. You know the kind--the one that holds pictures up to 3x5. That means they will also accomodate 3x5 cards, making them great to take on a research trip. Just write on the index cards problems on a certain person and slide it into the poly envelope, and when you get to the town where you ancestor lived, just look at your index cards to see what you need there. You can also make notes on the back of the card if you find the data needed. It's like taking along your own Rolodex file--only this one is flat and takes up less room.

Then there's the zip-loc type poly cases that are <u>very</u> handy to take with you any time you're diggin'. They hold pens, pencils, and change for the copy machine, etc. Remember that most places won't let you inside these days with your purse--too many valuable items have "walked out" of a library inside someone's pocketbook. Look carefully on the shelves at your discount store, and you'll see that some of these bags are three-hole-punched, to snap into a 3-ring notebook.

And what about Post-It pads? Although they come in all sizes, I prefer the small ones--stick them on everything. They don't tear your documents when removed later, like scotch tape would do. Suppose you have three families all mixed together in your files and want to sort them--put a Post-It on the front of a file folder, put the surname on it, and start sorting. Once everything is straightened out, you then remove the Post-It and stick it back on its pad to use again. And you still have an unmarked file folder to use for other things. You can use them for small notes to attach to the index cards in their poly envelopes (like, "check death date again"), or put them on papers you're working on at home (like, "check files for wife's name"), or to flag pages in a library book that you want to photocopy quickly when the machine is not in use. Post-Its are <u>not</u> for long-term use--they <u>do</u> leave damaging residue. And don't <u>ever</u> place one on old, original documents, for that reason.

So, the next time you're shopping at a discount store, or a five & dime, check out the school supply department and stock up on your needs. Only, don't tell Chuck I put you up to it, because you'll come home with a couple of bags of goodies (and nothing that you really went to buy!).

Write when you have time, and hugs to everyone.

Love,
Vera

CHRONOLOGICAL ORDER. The importance of listing every known event connected to an ancestor in chronological order.

{**v**}

Augusta, Georgia

Dear Bette,

     Everyone has certain ancestors who give them more trouble than the others, and the more data collected on them, the less you seem to know. You sit down and read all the material you've gathered, and get even more confused. This is where "chronology" becomes important!

     Whether you're a beginner, or a seasoned genealogist, you should periodically review your "problem child": and list in chronological order every event connected to him. This shows up what you can prove and, also, your weak points. It's very easy to do and goes like this:

1687..born Dorchester, Mass	1721..dau. born
1703..soldier..age 16	1722..moved to Scarboro, Maine
1712..married	1723..sold land in Wells, Maine
1714..dau. born	1723..bought land in Scarboro
1715..granted land in Maine	1724..bought more land
1716..dau. born	1734..dau. Abigail married
1717..dau. born	1735..dau. Mindwell married
1718..son Joseph born (mine)	1749..son Joseph married
1719..son born	1758..wife called "widow"

     This listing can go on and on, until you've listed everything known about this man. In the above chronology, I am missing the man's death record and his wife's death record, though it was between 1749, when he deeded land to son Joseph when he married, and 1758, when his wife was called a "widow" in the town records. And she died after 1763, when she sold off several acres of land she had inherited at her husband's death. These are my weak points!!

     Once a list of this kind is made, you then have at your fingertips a complete outline of your ancestor's "doings" during his lifetime. Not only that, it's a lot of fun just seeing how much you <u>do</u> know about him.

     Do one of your ancestors and send "old teacher" a copy so I can see how you do at it. Will be waiting for it.

Love,
Vera

DON'T MAKE STATEMENTS YOU CAN'T PROVE. A family history should include documentary evidence to substantiate each reference, such as marriages, deaths, and births.

{V}

Augusta, Georgia

Dear Bette,

Boy am I mad!! Have decided to take out my frustration on you, since it will give you another "don't you dare do this" lesson.

For two years my name has been on the waiting list for a book on one of my lines that is giving me trouble. It was described to me as "just what you need," and I was told that my line was in there. With all the glowing accounts given me, I had the idea it was the greatest thing in the world. HAH.

In all fairness, the book was beautifully written, and the family lines were very easy to follow. BUT, not a single piece of documentary evidence was given to substantiate these lines. There were no references, such as "this can be found in Vital Records of Roxbury, Massachusetts," no reproduced documents, such as death or marriage certificates. Nothing. Maybe when this book was written 50 years ago the author had seen, with his own eyes, these documents. But after all this time, I also want to see them! If references aren't listed in a book, how can you assure yourself that this is a correct lineage?

This is a mistake made by many authors of family histories. It's as if they're saying, "I wrote it, I published it, so it has to be true." This is the wrong attitude to take, as sometimes, years after your book comes out, new records are found which prove that you made a mistake. Of course you are gone by then, but think of the frustration others go through trying to find proof for your statements, when it didn't exist anywhere but in YOUR mind.

So the moral of this "lesson" is: When you decide to publish the family's history, don't make statements you can't prove. AND, if you can prove them, do it! Include references on where the material was found, and throw in copies of a few documents to make it interesting. It lets the reader know that you REALLY RESEARCHED the lines, and didn't make them up in your head. Frankly, I wouldn't give two cents for a family history that isn't fully documented and referenced! If you must research every aspect of the author's work, then why not just do your own "looking" from the start.

I feel much better now. As a cousin, you're the best (which means you let me yell at you!). Hope to hear from you again soon.

Love,
Vera

7

WARNING: "POT HOLE" DATES AHEAD! Simplest things in research often become "pot holes" in the research road--like system of writing and interpreting dates, for instance.

{V}

Augusta, Georgia

Dear Bette,

I just finished going through some old Massachusetts records transcriptions and decided that it is time to remind you about dates in your family papers. Remember to write each date like this: 20 Dec 1870. Do NOT use numbers to designate a month! It makes problems for anyone using your records later (boy, does it!).

Most records used by a beginning researcher have been transcribed or abstracted from the originals by someone else, and that's where the trouble starts for us. Fifty years later, we have no idea which dating system the compiler used, but we do know that many copiers substituted a number for the month. What difference would that make?? A lot, believe me!

Suppose a compiler listed dates as month, day, and year--10 Dec 1870 would be written 12/10/1870, or 12:10:1870. Very simple, right? BUT, suppose another compiler, using her own system, wrote her dates as day, month, and year--10 Dec 1870 now is written 10/12/1870. That's easy to understand, too (to her, anyway!). Now YOU, the reader of these records, come along and you read them in the same manner as you are used to writing them. So 12/10 now becomes 12 October. And you have just made an error in dating your records! This is where you must become a detective (remember, the first rule in genealogy, on your way to becoming a detective, is "Don't automatically assume anything!").

Before copying any dates from compiled records, you must first make sure which system of writing dates that particular compiler used. This is done by simply going through a few pages of the records. What are you looking for? You are looking for any number over 12 and determining where the compiler placed it. "Where" is the secret here, and the rest falls into place. Suppose you find dates written 28/6/1880, 15/11/1870, and 31/9/1872. What does that tell you? Well, knowing that there are only 12 months to a year, any number over 12 MUST designate the day. Now you have the system--this compiler writes her dates with the day first, and the month next.

If you will check each set of records that you're looking through to determine which system of writing dates the compiler used, your own records will be more accurate. And accuracy is what we're all striving towards!

Well, dear, that's it for today. Give my love to the family, and write soon.

Love,
Vera

{V}

Augusta, Georgia

Dear Bette,

Yes, I heard your area was having cold weather and I envy you!! The only way to describe how HOT it is here, is to say that it's the first time I've ever been able to POUR peanut butter right out of the jar!

After your letter came telling me how much you've accomplished on your lineage, I decided it was time for you to set up a Personal Index File. Otherwise, you'll be ruffling through page after page of charts saying "that name was here somewhere!" The file is simple and inexpensive to set up; later you can get fancy when there are three or four hundred names to keep track of.

One stop will do it--an office supply store. You want to buy 3x5 index cards, an index box (we women call them recipe boxes), a package of alphabetical divider cards, a stamp pad, and black stamp pad ink. Then, have the clerk order a rubber stamp that reads something like this:

NAME
BORN:
MARRIED:
SPOUSE:
CHART NO:
PERSON NO.

When the stamp arrives, use it to stamp on the blank side of the 3x5 cards. You're now ready to fill each card with an ancestor's data. Be sure to use either black ink to print on the cards, or a black ribbon to type on them. You may wish to photocopy these cards for someone else and blue ink will not copy well. Once you have all the ancestors listed, along with personal data, the cards are filed alphabetically in the box. Nice and easy, huh??

Don't forget that the CHART NO. and PERSON NO. refer to your Ancestor Charts. And, of course, your Family Group Sheets should have the same numbers (we talked about this before).

Space left at the bottom of the card may be used to list residence, occupation, a 2nd marriage, etc. The back, which is lined, may be used to list the children of this couple. Other notations may also be added, for example, after the person's name place (2) or (3) to indicate an additional marriage, and, there-fore, other cards for this person--or (Rev. War) for war service. Don't forget to use q.v.. "What's q.v.?" you ask. In Latin, it means "which see," and may be used when you have lineage sheets on a wife, also. And some family researchers use it to denote the child of our ancestor that WE are descended through. Sure beats having to follow each son to figure out which one is yours. Right??

When you write again, I expect to hear that you have started a file like this! It's amazing how much time (and wear and tear on your nerves) it will save you. More later.

Love,
Vera

9

FILE THEM AND KEEP THEM--ALL OF THEM! Until you're sure, very sure, that those bits and pieces of research notes aren't your lines, be a pack rat and keep them. One day they may be worth their weight in gold to you!

{v}

Augusta, Georgia

Dear Bette,

Just a short letter tonight as I'm exhausted from raking leaves all afternoon. I had something brought to my attention the other day and thought you needed to hear it, too. As you know, we can collect a lot of material on our surnames that doesn't seem to belong to our personal families. And if you're not the type (like me) to keep data that isn't useful to your research--it ends up in the trash. That is a NO NO!

A member of AGS, Helen Bredenberg Smith, was telling the story of her early research into her German ancestry. Some nice lady sent her reams of material on this surname, but, after going through all of it, Helen concluded that this wasn't information on her line, and since her files were already bulging with papers, she threw away these unneeded ones. Now, many years later, she has found that it not only was her line, but it concerned her direct line! And to make matters even worse, the lady who sent the material to her has passed away, and none of her family can be located.

The lesson learned from this story is--if you're going to research the family lines, then you have to become a pack rat!! Because all of us have thrown away material that we needed later on in our research, we then have to locate all those records again--and paying for them is costly! So, get yourself a file cabinet and start saving all those bits and pieces that are sent to you!

Hope the family is okay. Write soon, as I've missed hearing from you.

Love,
Vera

"ABRACADABRA" NUMBERING SYSTEMS. On the use of unintelligible numbering systems when putting together generations in a family history.

{V}

Augusta, Georgia

Dear Bette,

Boy, am I depressed and disgusted today!! Do you remember that Wheeler book that I've wanted to get my hands on for years? Well, the library found several places that had a copy, but since it's been out of print for years, no one would lend a copy out. That's understandable. If it got lost, it can't be replaced. But some of my friends have been keeping an eye out for it at every library they visit, and one of them wrote to say she'd located the book. I was on Cloud Nine for a week, then her next letter came. She'd found my David in the book, but she said the numbering system used by the author was so complex that she couldn't follow David forward, or backward. And she is an experienced researcher with 30 years of searching family histories! What a letdown that was!! Not only did I feel depressed, I was angry, too. Why do "they" go to the trouble of writing the family history, and then use a system that no one can understand? Why does an otherwise normal person go to all that trouble to confuse the reader he hopes will buy his book? It's beyond me.

Some systems are out of this world. They use only the letters of the alphabet, and after a few generations some of these combinations are really weird (and unprintable!). Why cause all this confusion? Why not use a system that would show you at a glance where to go next? There are such systems. One man I know (Gordon Randall) dealt with all the collateral lines in the second section of his book, all filed alphabetically--a simple method and one his readers will love. They are followed from the earliest known ancestor, down to the one who married into his family.

Another excellent system used by many professional genealogists is the "Register" system. With it, your earliest ancestor is #1. His children are 2, 3, 4, etc. If you've located your immigrant ancestor, then you can assign a superscript, which allows the reader to work backwards from any generation. For the superscript, using my line below, it looks like this:

Caleb^3, Nathan^2, Benjamin^1.

If you wish to check this system further, it is used in the New England Historical and Genealogical Society Register. This is not an open-ended system--if further children are found, a supplemental listing (e.g, 18a) must be devised. This system is difficult for a beginner to understand.

The numbering system I like best is the Henry System used by the Nye Family Association in their Genealogy of American Nye's of English Origin. This system is an open one, as each member has his own number. This number is his alone, no other family member will have it, ever. You're aware that you never find information on every descendant of a man, at least not right away, but you still want to print the book. What happens then, if you find data later and want to list this person in a supplement? The answer is simple: You give him his own personal number, and when you get the material on him, you use that number.

I'll show you how it works, using my Nye line: 1st generation, Benjamin; 2nd, Nathan; 3rd, Caleb; and 4th Benjamin. The 4th generation Benjamin Nye has the number "1793." Reading this number FROM RIGHT TO LEFT, he was the 3rd child of Caleb, who was the 9th child of Nathan, who was the 7th child of Benjamin, who was the first of our line to arrive in America. [I can hear you saying, "But what if Benjamin^4 had been the 10th child of Caleb, instead of the 3rd child of Caleb. Simple. Benjamin's number would be 179(10).] So, if you find your grandfather in the 8th generation with the number

"12345678," drop off the "8" in his number, and find the man in the 7th generation with the remaining numbers 1234567; your grandfather will be listed as his 8th child.

There are other simple systems to use, and it's the responsibility of the author to find one that suits his book. Otherwise, his readers will throw up their hands in defeat and never have the urge to buy the book on "their" family.

Hope everyone there is okay. Write when you have time.

Love,

Vere

WHAT TO DO WITH THOSE UNFINISHED LINES? Take your choice: Leave your notes in a mess, for others to throw away? Or, preserve your work so others can pick up where you left off? Here's what one researcher did. . .

{v}

Augusta, Georgia

Dear Bette,

Through the years we've talked about the many ways to preserve the family lines that are documented back to the immigrant ancestor. But we've never talked about the other lines, the ones you've never been able to complete no matter how much time you spent in research. We all have such lines, with loads of material in the files, and don't quite know what to do with it all. We're getting older, our eyes are going, our ability to travel is going, added family responsibilities need attention--whatever the reason, everything points to our not being able to finish what we started.

So, what happens to our years of research? Do we leave it, in a mess, for others to throw away? Or, do we try to put in in order so it can be completed by others? If you choose the first way, then all your notes will be lost and others will have to start as you did--from the beginning. The obvious choice is to preserve your work so that others can pick up where you left off and go on from there. Right? And that is just what one of our AGS members has done.

Troup Morton, one of our most dedicated members and a super genealogist, some time ago published a beautifully-put-together book on the Morton family, From Plymouth Rock to Pine Ridge, a well-documented story of the Mortons' emigration from Massachusetts to Georgia. Then he went to work on one of his mother's lines, the Buck family, also from "Up North." But he is too far from primary sources to complete the line at this time. Recently, he placed in our library a compilation of data on William Buck of Pitt County, North Carolina, and of Washington County, Georgia. The format used is almost identical to the one used by us all for completed lines, with one important exception: the statement made at the very beginning, "this compilation is based upon incomplete research." This lets each reader of his work know that more data is needed if this line is to be completed.

Some would say that if your work isn't finished, why go to all the trouble of getting it together in book form? The answer to that question lies in Troup's own words, "the justification for the compilation is that it may be used to preserve the extent of present investigation and enable future inquiry by later generations." That says it all! And better than I could!

His compilation, in a durable pressboard binder, is set up beautifully for the reader, with all the research done and all the documents collected, right there at your finger tips. There are family charts, with everything that could be found listed on them, along with explanations of how and were the data was located.

There is a section of maps showing the lands owned by the Buck family in both states (what a great idea!). And, finally, there are appendixes, which consist of deed copies and abstracts, Civil War military service, selected pages from diaries, several family charts showing descendants of William Buck, and abstracts of family records and correspondence. He also included photocopied family portraits.

He gave credit, by name, to all those researchers who had contributed data from their own files through the years, and, in so doing, had helped him compile this material. All of this seems like a lot of work, and it is! But when you consider the alternative, years of work thrown away, then I think we all must follow Troup's example and put our files in order.

Well, dear, must close for now, hope to hear from you soon, and hugs to all.

Love,
Vera

WHERE THERE'S A WILL, THERE'S A WAY! You should make provisions for your research data; the alternative may be having years of work wind up at the city dump!

{V}

Augusta, Georgia

Dear Bette,

We're going to have a heart-to-heart talk today about something very important, although I hadn't realized it before. I stopped at a friend's house last week and found her in hysterics. By the time she calmed down and told me the trouble, I was in hysterics!

She has been a family researcher for over 30 years, and her husband had said to her, "Joan, why don't you stop all this nonsense, you've spent most of your time for years, and a lot of money, on this junk. It's such a waste--when you die it will all end up at the dump."

Her question was, "What can I do?" We found the answer after much thought. After going home, I sat in my office looking at everything I'd collected in the past 40 years, picturing it at the dump--and knowing that I couldn't let that happen. My husband isn't interested in family research, either; his theory is, "If they're dead, let them rest in peace." So, I'm going to tell you what we did, what you should do, and what you should tell all your friends to do.

I have added a codicil to my will stating that the contents of my file cabinets, all my ledgers, all my books, anything at all pertaining to research, is to be given to the Augusta Genealogical Society. I have included a letter to the Society, requesting that they photocopy all the papers concerning my direct line, and then send the originals to my niece. I've also asked that, if it's possible, a copy of my Marshall and Munson family research be placed in the Maine State Library. This last request would complete one of my dreams: both families "came out of" Maine and neither one has ever been "done," therefore, there is nothing to be found in Maine by their descendants.

Now, everyone doesn't like to do the same things (that would be boring!), so you can't fault the members of your family for not being interested in genealogy. But you can, and you MUST, protect the material you have so painstakingly collected through the years. And you owe it to future generations of these families to put your material out in the "public eye," so they can use it when they have been bitten by the "bug" that bit you. Wherever you live, there is a genealogical society just sitting there waiting for YOUR research papers. If there isn't, there's always a state library in the state where your family originated, and they would love to have your papers.

So, I expect to hear, in your next letter, that you have followed our lead, and done something to protect your papers after you're gone (that's an order, kiddo!!). The alternative is rather scary!

That's enough bossing around for now, so will close with

Love,
Vera

YOUR CHOICE: FOREVER--OR TO THE DUMP? "Being of sound mind and body" was the way our ancestors began putting their affairs in order. Your descendants will appreciate <u>your</u> being of "sound mind" right now by putting your family files in order. Else, to the dump!

{V}

Augusta, Georgia

Dear Bette,

The last time we talked you said that you were "considering" my advice to put all your family research into some permanent form. Have you started yet?? I hope that you have, as it's important to do this as we go along. Many of us get so involved in the actual research that we never take time to get our material into some form that others could understand after we're gone.

Our descendants, then faced with file after file of jumbled records, will head for the nearest dump! So we owe it to them to straighten out our work while we can. Doing this also helps <u>us</u>; many times I've found notes in my files that I'd forgotten were there--and I was <u>still</u> searching for these documents! If you sort your files and data periodically, you save yourself extra work! START NOW!!

Recently one of our AGS members, Flora Belknap of Sun City, Arizona, presented our Augusta Genealogical Society library with her lifetime collection of family research. And what a collection! The gift list alone is four pages long! Each family is complete in its own folder, and all done so beautifully that all our staff needs to do is to index them. As Flora completed a family, she placed all records pertaining to that family together. Group sheets, ancestor charts, deeds, wills, birth, death, and marriage records, cemetery records, tax lists, military records, and on and on. Everything she had found to document that particular family was in that file, and each family had been researched thoroughly. Future researchers using this collection are going to bless the day that Flora caught the genealogy "bug"!! Never have I seen a collection put together so beautifully--and it's a definite asset to our AGS library, thanks to Flora!

My dear, why don't you use Flora as an example and begin sorting <u>your</u> material <u>now</u>. It isn't sensible to wait "until I get everything," because that may take years. In the meantime, your files make sense only to you (and not always to you). Label file folders with each of your surnames and then start sorting--everything pertaining to that surname goes in its own file. Once that's done, you can sort each folder into generations--this will also point out to you the documents you still need to complete this line. From there, you line up the proofs that go with each ancestor, the children, grandchildren, etc., and there you have your basic file. It will be refined as you get more data, but right now you have all information pertaining to any one surname all in one place. No more rambling through 15 file folders saying, "Now <u>where</u> did I put Aunt Jane's death?"

You might want to rearrange the file cabinet, too, labeling folders with surnames instead of whatever they have on them now. When I bought my first cabinet years ago I set up this system--each folder had a surname on it, and surnames were filed alphabetically in each drawer. At the time, I didn't have the brains to know that I was doing something smart, but it has saved me loads of time while searching out data for others.

Well, time to start cooking again (my next house <u>will</u> <u>not</u> have a kitchen!!). Write when you have time, and give my love to the kids.

Love,
Vera

ORDER--OR CHAOS? If something happened to a family historian, would the family know what to do with the material gathered over several years? Is it "junk" or a treasure of information? Moral: Put your papers in order now!

{V}

Augusta, Georgia

Dear Bette,

That was a good question. No, you should _not_ wait until you can prove every single line before putting together a family history.

A friend of mine has a method I like. Every time she completes about four generations (approximately 100 years) on her family and allied lines, she puts it together in manuscript form. Denise says it's easy and goes like this:

She types a "fact sheet" on the male ancestor, wife, parents, and children. Behind that she lines up the documents proving the lineage. Then she places photos of the people, their homes, and their tombstones; birth, marriage, and death records; deeds, wills, and any other material she has. For the female ancestor, she lists the maiden name (of course) and all _her_ data and then she puts the notation "see MacLean family." At the end of the manuscript, she has a section of all the allied lines who married into _her_ family. These are filed alphabetically by surname and are traced as far back as she has been able to go.

This may not be everyone's "cup of tea" as to method, but, at least when she has passed away, her descendants won't wonder "what do do with all this stuff." It is completed in sections--that's the important thing. So many of us get so wrapped up in searching that we forget to put our research material in some kind of order. Just because _we_ know that great-aunt Lizzie was famous for her poetry doesn't mean that others will--IF WE DON'T TELL THEM! That's our responsibility to our descendants: to leave papers that they can understand, and not just bits and pieces that don't make sense.

Many children give their parents' family papers to historical and genealogical societies because they don't know what to do with them. Several years ago, in our hometown, the historical society was moving to larger quarters and down in the basement they found boxes galore of papers given to them by the son of a prominent man in town. These boxes had been there for a very long time and had never been sorted. They got quite a shock when they began going through them!! Inside was every imaginable historical paper you could think of: letters between George Washington and his commanders; the planning of some battles; some personal correspondence. Here were unknown signatures from famous men, now seen for the first time! In all, they'd had a gold mine in the basement for years.

The moral of this story is: not everyone has the time nor the knowledge to sort out and put papers in order. If you want them used in future years, then you must do the "putting in order." So do as Denise has. Set up the number of generations you want to include, and type it up! NOW!! Bossy, aren't I?

Love,
Vera

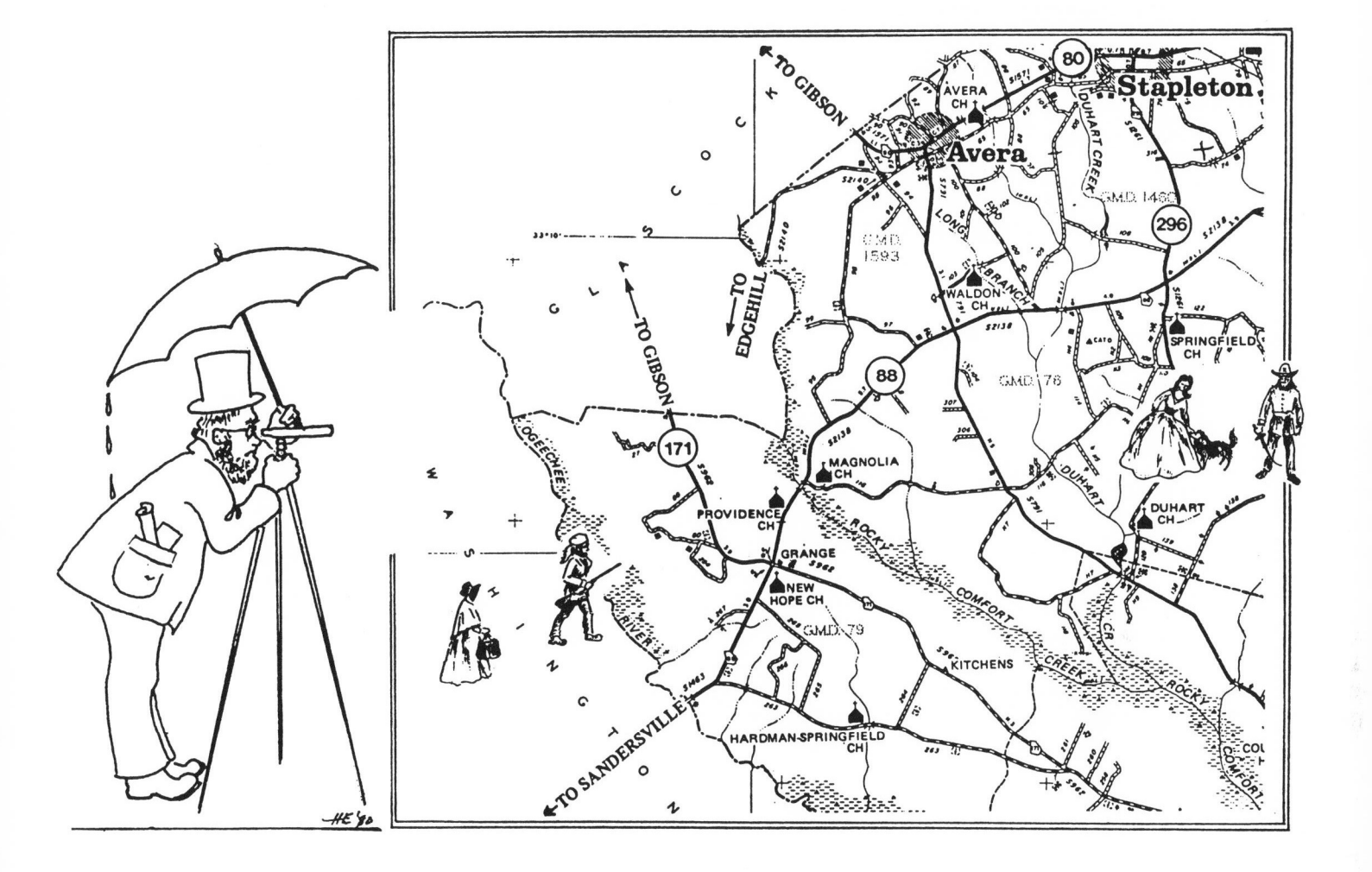

Chapter 2

Charting a Course on the Research Road

*An ancestor chart is your research road map;
a family group sheet is a major stop along
that road. And there are other "up and down"
charts to show each limb on your family tree.*

ANCESTOR CHARTS. There aren't many times in life when <u>you</u> are <u>always</u> #1, but this is one of them! The numbering system goes on to assign all males in your line even numbers, and all females odd (wouldn't you know??) numbers. It's neat!

{V}   Augusta, Georgia

Dear Bette,

Today, let's talk about the Ancestor (Pedigree) Chart, another direct-blood-line chart. They can be bought with four, five, or even fifteen generations to a page. In my opinion, these are <u>the</u> most important charts in your files, as once completely filled in, each ancestor has his/her own personal number, and this number can be entered on every paper in your files pertaining to that particular ancestor (doing this simplifies things for you, particularly if you have several ancestors with the same name, like John Smith. This personal number marked on a will shows you immediately which John it belongs to. Neat, huh?).

On your Ancestor Chart you are always Number 1. Your father is #2 and your mother is #3. From there on, it's simply a matter of doubling each number to identify that person's father...and then "plus 1" to identify the father's wife.

Thus your paternal grandfather is #4 and your paternal great-grandfather is #8, while your paternal grandmother is #5 (4 + 1) and your paternal great-grandmother is #9 (8 + 1). This system automatically puts all your father's lines on the top half of the page and your mother's on the bottom half. Oh yes, notice that all males have even numbers, and all females un-even ones (notice, too, that I didn't say <u>odd</u> numbers!).

It's easier to show you, so I'm sending my own chart. Using the system I just described, our maternal grandfather, George Oscar Nye, has a personal number of 12. See where #12 is at the right? From there, he is "carried over" to the far left-hand position on a new chart (where I am on this chart) with the #1 spot changed to "12." Then his ancestry is carried on in the same way, with his father (#24) in the same slot as my #2 is.

A neat part of this numbering system (assigning permanent numbers, in a methodical way, to each ancestor) is that it makes it easy to draw up an ahnentafel, one of the most efficient search aids you'll ever use. I'll save <u>that</u> lesson to next time.

Love,
Vera

8 Charles William Marshall
b. 24 Aug. 1840
p.b. Port Clyde, ME
m. 30 Aug. 1864
p.m. St. George, ME
d. 4 May 1916
p.d. Calais, ME

4 William James Marshall (Father of No. 2)
b. 10 Aug. 1867
p.b. Calais, ME
m. 18 Sept. 1892
p.m. Calais, ME
d. 24 July 1956
p.d. Newton, CT

9 Mary Ann Thompson
b. 12 May 1847
p.b. St. George, ME
d. 20 Dec. 1923
p.d. Calais, ME

2 Bertrum Freeman Marshall (Father of No. 1)
b. 6 Apr. 1894
p.b. Calais, ME
m. 19 Feb. 1917
p.m. New York City, NY
d. 9 June 1949
p.d. Derby, CT

10 Alfred Douglas Munson
b. 4 July 1852
p.b. St. George, N.B. Canada
m. 10 Nov. 1872
p.m. Charlotte Co., N.B.
d. 4 May 1932
p.d. Milltown (bur. Calais), ME

5 Florence Margaret Munson (Mother of No. 2)
b. 26 Feb. 1874
p.b. St. Stephen, N.B. Canada
d. 27 Apr. 1928
p.d. West Haven, CT

11) Elvira Ruth McClaskey
b.
p.b.
d. in childbirth..1878
p.d. prob. Calais = Milltown, ME

1 Vera Marion Marshall
b. 3 Jan. 1929
p.b. Shelton, CT
m. 25 May 1947
p.m. North Augusta, SC
d.
p.d.

12 George Oscar Nye
b. 17 Oct. 1844
p.b. Dudley, MA
m. 3 Jan. 1869
p.m.
d. 19 Aug. 1892
p.d. Manchester, NH

6 George Henry Nye (Father of No. 3)
b. 31 Jan. 1872
p.b. New Haven, CT
m. 19 Feb. 1893
p.m. New York City, NY
d. 26 June 1954
p.d. New Haven, CT

13 Marion M. Covert
b. 3 Jan. 1845
p.b. Croton, NY
d. 27 July 1921
p.d. West Haven, CT

3 Bertha Amelia Nye (Mother of No. 1)
b. 16 Mar. 1897
p.b. New Haven, CT
d. 26 May 1946
p.d. New Haven, CT

14 Francis Marion Bristol
b. 22 Feb. 1844
p.b. New Haven, CT
m. 24 Dec. 1868
p.m.
d. 19 Sept. 1912
p.d. Plainville, CT

7 Cora Mae Bristol (Mother of No. 3)
b. 22 Feb. 1876
p.b. Meriden, CT
d. 22 June 1959
p.d. Hamden, CT

15 Amelia Elizabeth Polley
b. 20 Mar. 1852
p.b. New Britain, CT
d. 21 Nov. 1893
p.d. Cheshire, CT

EACH BLANK IS A MYSTERY TO SOLVE. An <u>ahnentafel</u> is a table devised by those efficient Germans to keep track of all your ancestors in a methodical way.

{V}

Augusta, Georgia

Dear Bette,

      Several years ago, I said the same thing to a friend of mine that your latest letter asks me, "How can you keep track of so many ancestors and still know who belongs where?" She showed me the method she uses and it's GREAT! It's called an <u>ahnentafel</u> (no, I didn't hit the wrong keys). This is a German word and the literal translation means "ancestor table." You can follow any ancestor simply by taking his or her number and multiplying it by two. This gives you the person's father. Then use the same procedure to find the next generation. Take ancestor No. 6. His father is No. 12 and his mother is No. 13 (wives are always their husband's number plus one). No. 12's father would be No. 24, and so on. Just like on ancestor charts that you're familiar with, the same rule applies here, too--even numbers are males and uneven numbers are females. I'll show you how it works, beginning with your father.

Name	When & Where Born	When & Where Died
1. Everett C. Ludington	1893 Hartford Co., CT	1978 Orange Co., FL
2. Myron E. Ludington	1866 Hampshire Co., MA	1936 New Haven Co., CT
3. Eva E. Crane	1871 Hartford Co., CT	1955 Okeechobee Co., FL
4. Augustine Ludington	1835 Hampden Co., MA	1910 Hampden Co., MA
5. Harriet Russell	1829 Hampden Co., MA	1917 Hampden Co., MA
6. Curtis L. Crane	1845 Hartford Co., CT	1922 Hartford Co., CT
7. Celia M. Johnson	1844 Hampden Co., MA	1930 Hartford Co., CT
8. Jason P. Ludington	1787 Hampden Co., MA	1865 Hampden Co., MA
9. Princess (Danks) Wolcott	1798 Hampden Co., MA	1860 Hampden Co., MA
10.		
11.		
12. Lorenzo B. Crane	1818 Hartford Co., CT	1892 Hartford Co., CT
13. Emeline Gowdy	1820 Tolland Co., CT	Hartford Co., CT
14.		
15.		
16. Daniel Ludington	1751 Hampden Co., MA	1824 Hampden Co., MA
17. Naomi Searle	1755 Hampshire Co., MA	

      This table can continue back as far as you have proven your ancestry. If you had begun with yourself as No. 1, then this table would include your paternal <u>and</u> maternal lines, and could run into several pages--but it's worth every bit of your time and trouble. Here at your finger tips, you have each ancestor known to you, plus his vital statistics. (You may also want to add marriage place and date to your table, space permitting.) But better than that, you also have all the blank spaces right in front of you where the lines need more work. Nos. 10, 11, 14, and 15 are blank, the death record for No. 17 is blank, so now you can see that you need to find the parents for Harriet Russell (No. 5) and also for Celia Johnson (No. 7), and you need to find out where Naomi Searle died.

      The very best thing about fixing up a table like this is that you now have something to take with you on your research trips. Never (!) go to the archives, the state library (or to <u>any</u> library, for that matter), cemetery hunting, or to the courthouse without your <u>ahnentafel</u> in your folder. Each blank space is a new mystery to solve, showing which dates are needed and which counties and states would be most likely to have what you need. So, get out the typewriter and get busy, kid. I expect to see a sample from you soon.

      Hugs and kisses for the family, and hope you put us on your "visit list" this year.

Love,
Vera

FAMILY GROUP NO. 4   Husband's Full Name   WILLIAM JAMES MARSHALL

This information Obtained From:	Husband's Data	Day Month Year	City, Town or Place	County or Province, etc.	State or Country	Add. Info. on Husband
Birth, Marriage, Death,	Birth	10 Aug. 1867	Calais	Washington	ME	SS No.
& Cemetery Records for	Chr'nd					049-01-6912
all towns mentioned	Marr.	18 Sep. 1892	Calais	Washington	ME	
	Death	24 July 1956	Newton	Fairfield	CT	
Census, 1870 - 1910	Burial		Huntington		CT	Lawn Cem.
	Places of Residence	Calais, ME, Marlboro, MA, Shelton, CT				
Obits from newspapers	Occupation Watchman		Church Affiliation Baptist		Military Rec.	
	Other wives, if any. No. (1) (2) etc. Make separate sheet for each marr.					
	His Father Chas. Wm. Marshall			Mother's Maiden Name Mary Ann Thompson		

Wife's Full Maiden Name   FLORENCE MARGARET MUNSON

	Wife's Data	Day Month Year	City, Town or Place	County or Province, etc	State or Country	Add. Info. on Wife
	Birth	26 Feb. 1874	St. Stephen	Charlotte, N.B. Canada		
	Chr'nd					
	Death	27 Apr. 1928	West Haven		CT	
	Burial		Huntington		CT	Lawn Cem.
Compiler Vera M. McDowell	Places of Residence	same as husband				
Address 2307 Harding Rd.	Occupation		Church Affiliation		Military Rec.	
City, State Augusta, GA 30906	Other husbands, if any. No. (1) (2) etc. Make separate sheet for each marr.					
Date 15 Aug. 1967	Her Father Alfred D. Munson			Mother's Maiden Name Elvira McClaskey		

Sex	Children's Names in Full (Arrange in order of birth)	Children's Data	Day Month Year	City, Town or Place	County or Province, etc.	State or Country	Add. info. on Children
	1 Bertrum Freeman *	Birth	6 Apr. 1894	Calais	Washington	ME	
		Marr.	19 Feb. 1917	New York City		NY	
	Full Name of Spouse	Death	9 Jun. 1949	Derby		CT	
	Bertha Amelia Nye	Burial	11 Jun. 1949	Derby		CT	Oak Cliff Cem.
	2 Queena S.	Birth	15 Jul. 1897	Calais	Washington	ME	
		Marr.	bef. 1918				son Walter,
	Full Name of Spouse	Death	Sep. 1924	New Haven		CT	Jr. b. Dec.
	Walter Corbiere	Burial					1918
	3 Arvilla	Birth	1902	Calais	Washington	ME	
		Marr.					
	Full Name of Spouse	Death	1904	Marlboro		MA	
		Burial					
	4 Ruth Helen Arvilla	Birth	9 Feb. 1904	Marlboro		MA	no ch.
		Marr.	19 Feb. 1948	Philadelphia		PA	
	Full Name of Spouse	Death	18 Jan. 1978	Hamden		CT	Ruth a
	Rev. Frank Hoar	Burial		Zarapheth		NJ	minister
	5 Otis Vincent	Birth	4 Oct. 1915	Marlboro		MA	also 3 more
		Marr.					wives
	Full Name of Spouse	Death					2 daus.
	4) Arlene Jones	Burial					
	6	Birth					
		Marr.					
	Full Name of Spouse	Death					
		Burial					
	7	Birth					
		Marr.					
	Full Name of Spouse	Death					
		Burial					
	8	Birth					
		Marr.					
	Full Name of Spouse	Death					
		Burial					
	9	Birth					
		Marr.					
	Full Name of Spouse	Death					
		Burial					

Form A1. Family Group Sheet by The Everton Publishers, P.O. Box 368, Logan, UT 84321. Publishers of *The Genealogical Helper*. Send for a free catalogue with list and full descriptions of many genealogical aids.

FAMILY GROUP SHEETS: STOPS ALONG THE RESEARCH ROAD. If your ancestor chart is a "road map" for your genealogical research, consider the family group sheet a major stop along the way. <u>There</u> you'll find the siblings who <u>may</u> have the family Bible!!

{*v*}

Augusta, Georgia

Dear Bette,

This will be just a quickie as I've got to cut the yard before it gets too hot. I was thinking about you last night and realized that there is another important subject we'd never talked about--family group sheets (yes dear, another chart!!). I've enclosed one of mine so that you can see just how much they're needed to keep our families straight in our files.

If you recall, on your ahnentafel , #4 was your grandfather (also on your ancestor chart), so this is a family group sheet on <u>my</u> grandfather, his wife, and children. All the vital information you've collected on each family member is listed on this sheet, including the references for the sources of that information. The family group number on these sheets corresponds to the same number on your ancestor chart and ahnentafel (father #2, gr-grandfather #8, etc.). Since the females all have odd numbers, note that my grandmother is #5 (making <u>her</u> father #10--a father is always double the number of his child). See how simple it is to keep records this way!! My direct-line notebook has one of these sheets at the beginning of every generation, and they are lined up numerically with <u>my</u> father (#2) on the first page, and his documentation follows that (birth, death, etc.).

We all collect data on the siblings of each ancestor--it can be kept straight in our notebooks by using these same sheets. The family group number would be the father's number, followed by the number of the child. As an example: using the chart I've sent, notice that Queena is the second child--her family group sheet would be numbered 4/2; Ruth's would be 4/4 and Otis' would be 4/5. Any time you see this <u>double</u> <u>number</u> on a chart you know it isn't your direct line, but you would immediately know how it fits into your family when you check your ahnentafel to see who the number on the left belongs to (grandpa's kids).

You'll notice that I didn't mention child #1--<u>his</u> family group number <u>is</u> <u>not</u> 4/1. The asterisk placed by the name of Bertrum shows that this is my direct line, so as my father, his group sheet carries the number <u>2</u> (see my ahnentafel I sent you).

Filling in these charts is a lot of work, but once done they save a researcher loads of time. Start on your own family and see how much easier it is to locate someone in your records (Yes, NOW!!).

Must get busy so will close for now. Hugs to you both and to the kids.

Love,
Vera

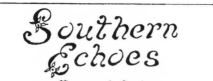

Southern Echoes
Monograph Series
Special Publication Number One

Originally published by the
Augusta Genealogical Society, Inc.
Augusta, Georgia
Copyright © 1992 by the Augusta
Genealogical Society, Inc.
All Rights Reserved

Reprinted 1995 by the
Genealogical Publishing Co., Inc.
1001 N. Calvert St., Baltimore, Md. 21202
Second printing 1996
Third printing 1997

Library of Congress Catalogue Card Number 95-78281
International Standard Book Number 0-8063-1484-2
Made in the United States of America

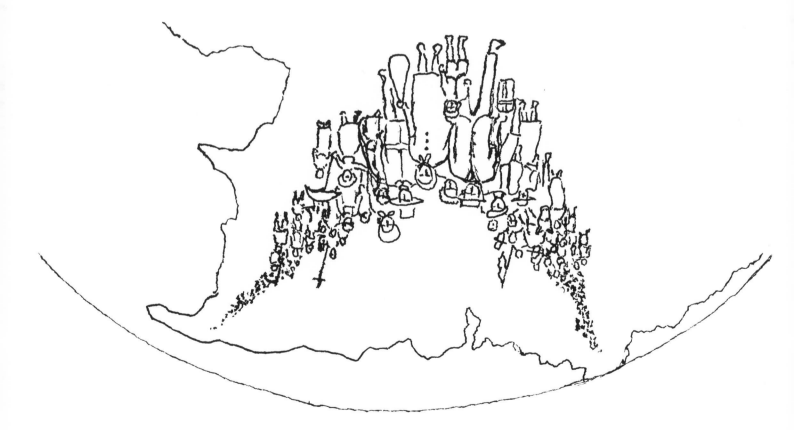

Chapter 1

Getting the Record Straight

Order--or Chaos? All depends on getting your notes and files organized. Don't, and it's Chaos! Keep your files simple and open-ended, and for Heaven's sake, document as you go along--*that's* Order.

PERSONAL INDEX FILE. Setting up an easy filing system on ancestors saves time--and wear and tear on nerves!

{V}

Augusta, Georgia

Dear Bette,

Yes, I heard your area was having cold weather and I envy you!! The only way to describe how HOT it is here, is to say that it's the first time I've ever been able to POUR peanut butter right out of the jar!

After your letter came telling me how much you've accomplished on your lineage, I decided it was time for you to set up a Personal Index File. Otherwise, you'll be ruffling through page after page of charts saying "that name was here somewhere!" The file is simple and inexpensive to set up; later you can get fancy when there are three or four hundred names to keep track of.

One stop will do it--an office supply store. You want to buy 3x5 index cards, an index box (we women call them recipe boxes), a package of alphabetical divider cards, a stamp pad, and black stamp pad ink. Then, have the clerk order a rubber stamp that reads something like this:

NAME
BORN:
MARRIED:
SPOUSE:
CHART NO:
PERSON NO.

When the stamp arrives, use it to stamp on the blank side of the 3x5 cards. You're now ready to fill each card with an ancestor's data. Be sure to use either black ink to print on the cards, or a black ribbon to type on them. You may wish to photocopy these cards for someone else and blue ink will not copy well. Once you have all the ancestors listed, along with personal data, the cards are filed alphabetically in the box. Nice and easy, huh??

Don't forget that the CHART NO. and PERSON NO. refer to your Ancestor Charts. And, of course, your Family Group Sheets should have the same numbers (we talked about this before).

Space left at the bottom of the card may be used to list residence, occupation, a 2nd marriage, etc. The back, which is lined, may be used to list the children of this couple. Other notations may also be added, for example, after the person's name place (2) or (3) to indicate an additional marriage, and, there-fore, other cards for this person--or (Rev. War) for war service. Don't forget to use q.v.. "What's q.v.?" you ask. In Latin, it means "which see," and may be used when you have lineage sheets on a wife, also. And some family researchers use it to denote the child of our ancestor that WE are descended through. Sure beats having to follow each son to figure out which one is yours. Right??

When you write again, I expect to hear that you have started a file like this! It's amazing how much time (and wear and tear on your nerves) it will save you. More later.

Love,
Vera

"ABRACADABRA" NUMBERING SYSTEMS. On the use of unintelligible numbering systems when putting together generations in a family history.

{V}

Augusta, Georgia

Dear Bette,

Boy, am I depressed and disgusted today!! Do you remember that Wheeler book that I've wanted to get my hands on for years? Well, the library found several places that had a copy, but since it's been out of print for years, no one would lend a copy out. That's understandable. If it got lost, it can't be replaced. But some of my friends have been keeping an eye out for it at every library they visit, and one of them wrote to say she'd located the book. I was on Cloud Nine for a week, then her next letter came. She'd found my David in the book, but she said the numbering system used by the author was so complex that she couldn't follow David forward, or backward. And she is an experienced researcher with 30 years of searching family histories! What a letdown that was!! Not only did I feel depressed, I was angry, too. Why do "they" go to the trouble of writing the family history, and then use a system that no one can understand? Why does an otherwise normal person go to all that trouble to confuse the reader he hopes will buy his book? It's beyond me.

Some systems are out of this world. They use only the letters of the alphabet, and after a few generations some of these combinations are really weird (and unprintable!). Why cause all this confusion? Why not use a system that would show you at a glance where to go next? There are such systems. One man I know (Gordon Randall) dealt with all the collateral lines in the second section of his book, all filed alphabetically--a simple method and one his readers will love. They are followed from the earliest known ancestor, down to the one who married into his family.

Another excellent system used by many professional genealogists is the "Register" system. With it, your earliest ancestor is #1. His children are 2, 3, 4, etc. If you've located your immigrant ancestor, then you can assign a superscript, which allows the reader to work backwards from any generation. For the superscript, using my line below, it looks like this:

Caleb^3, Nathan^2, Benjamin^1.

If you wish to check this system further, it is used in the New England Historical and Genealogical Society Register. This is not an open-ended system--if further children are found, a supplemental listing (e.g, 18a) must be devised. This system is difficult for a beginner to understand.

The numbering system I like best is the Henry System used by the Nye Family Association in their Genealogy of American Nye's of English Origin. This system is an open one, as each member has his own number. This number is his alone, no other family member will have it, ever. You're aware that you never find information on every descendant of a man, at least not right away, but you still want to print the book. What happens then, if you find data later and want to list this person in a supplement? The answer is simple: You give him his own personal number, and when you get the material on him, you use that number.

I'll show you how it works, using my Nye line: 1st generation, Benjamin; 2nd, Nathan; 3rd, Caleb; and 4th Benjamin. The 4th generation Benjamin Nye has the number "1793." Reading this number FROM RIGHT TO LEFT, he was the 3rd child of Caleb, who was the 9th child of Nathan, who was the 7th child of Benjamin, who was the first of our line to arrive in America. [I can hear you saying, "But what if Benjamin^4 had been the 10th child of Caleb, instead of the 3rd child of Caleb. Simple. Benjamin's number would be 179(10).] So, if you find your grandfather in the 8th generation with the number

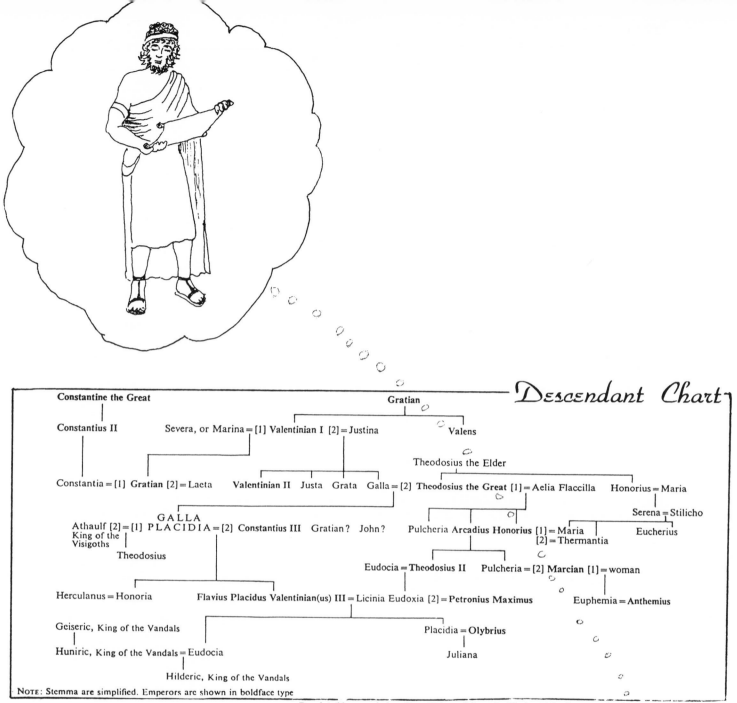

Descendant Chart

Constantine the Great

Gratian

Constantius II

Severa, or Marina = [1] Valentinian I [2] = Justina   Valens

Theodosius the Elder

Constantia = [1] Gratian [2] = Laeta   Valentinian II   Justa   Grata   Galla = [2] Theodosius the Great [1] = Aelia Flaccilla   Honorius = Maria

Serena = Stilicho

GALLA
Athaulf [2] = [1] PLACIDIA = [2] Constantius III   Gratian?   John?   Pulcheria Arcadius Honorius [1] = Maria   Eucherius
King of the   [2] = Thermantia
Visigoths

Theodosius

Eudocia = Theodosius II   Pulcheria = [2] Marcian [1] = woman

Herculanus = Honoria   Flavius Placidus Valentinian(us) III = Licinia Eudoxia [2] = Petronius Maximus   Euphemia = Anthemius

Geiseric, King of the Vandals   Placidia = Olybrius

Huniric, King of the Vandals = Eudocia   Juliana

Hilderic, King of the Vandals

NOTE: Stemma are simplified. Emperors are shown in boldface type

Reprinted by permission, from Chicago Manual of Style, 13th ed., rev. and enl. (Chicago, 1982), 339.

{v}

Augusta, Georgia

Dear Bette,

Today, I want to show you something new. Well, not <u>really</u> new, nothing in the research business is new, only new to us. During my years of Munson family research, I've found many "umpteenth removed" cousins. Some are of different generations and some are of a different child of another marriage. But we ALL descend from a common ancestor! So that each of us would know how the others "fit" into the family, we exchanged charts exactly like one I ran across the other day (and I thought <u>we</u> had invented it!).

Remember that the Romans were big on family trees (see, I told you there's nothing new under the sun!). The chart I'm enclosing shows Gratian's family (no wonder they were big on genealogy--they didn't have surnames to contend with!); I asked permission of the University of Chicago Press to reproduce it, so you and I can talk about it. Notice all the "goodies" found on this Descendant Chart that aren't available on any of the other charts we all use. If your ancestor was married more than once, all his wives are listed on this chart, and note that it shows which marriage <u>your</u> line comes down through. And see in the top left corner how you can show the ancestry of a person who married into your family.

The thing I like best about <u>this</u> chart is that it shows relationships in a family over several generations. You can see exactly the relationship between cousins who married cousins. If you take a good look at this chart, you'll be able to see where Theodosius the Great's grandson through a second marriage married T. the Great's great-granddaughter through a first marriage. Translate that on your own chart to ggg-g'father Smith's descendants, and you'll see how clear it is! Can you imagine having all this information available to you on just one chart? With other charts, we have to sort out multiple marriages and then line up all the charts on a table--just to be able to sort out the relationships that are ALL shown on the one chart below.

Well, dear that's it for this time. Draw up your own Descendant Chart using one of <u>your</u> ancestral lines and see how much fun it is. My love to the family.

Love,
Vera

PS: Decided to enclose samples of two more kinds of charts. The Fan Chart is one completed by our society's artist, Harry Evans. The Photo Chart visually traces Jerry Scott's son's lines. Jerry is our society's official photographer. These charts are for framing and display, and they're beautiful!

Photo Chart

1. Robert Mitchell Scott
2. Ralph Carter Scott, Sr.
3. Marjorie Priscilla Rugge
4. Ralph Clifton Scott
5. Agnes Cone
6. Frederick William Rugge
7. Mabelle F. G. McMurray
8. John Oliver Scott
9. Theodosia Earnest Shanklin
10. George Wilson Cone
11. Rebecca Ann Haseltine Carter
12. Hermann Rugge
13. Catharina Bischoff
14. James Edward McMurray
15. Eliza Ann Mitchell

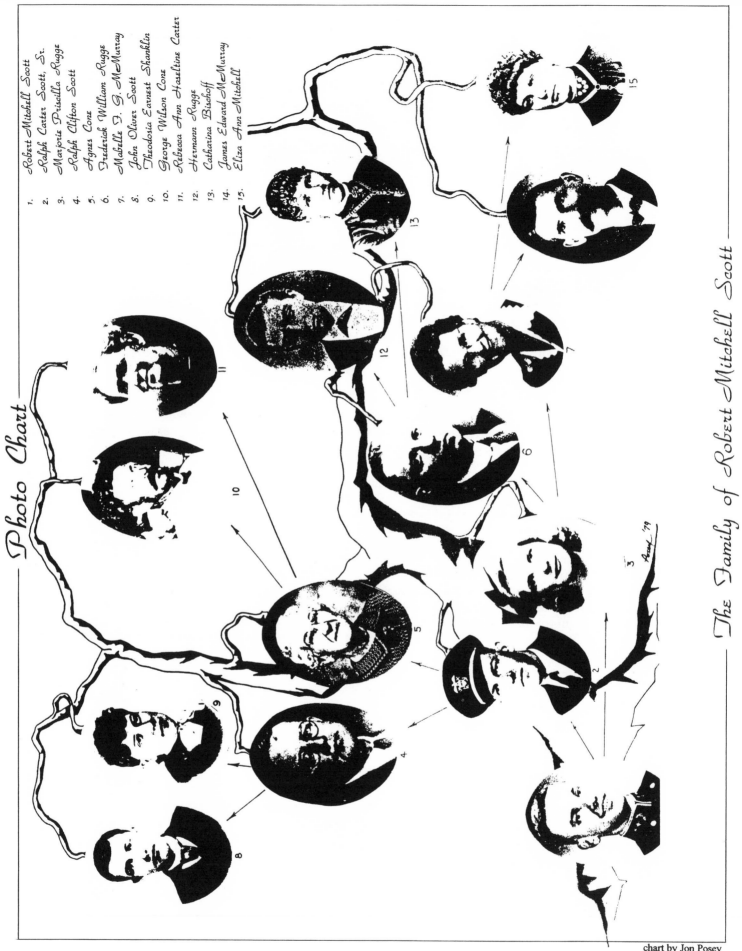

The Family of Robert Mitchell Scott

chart by Jon Posey

24

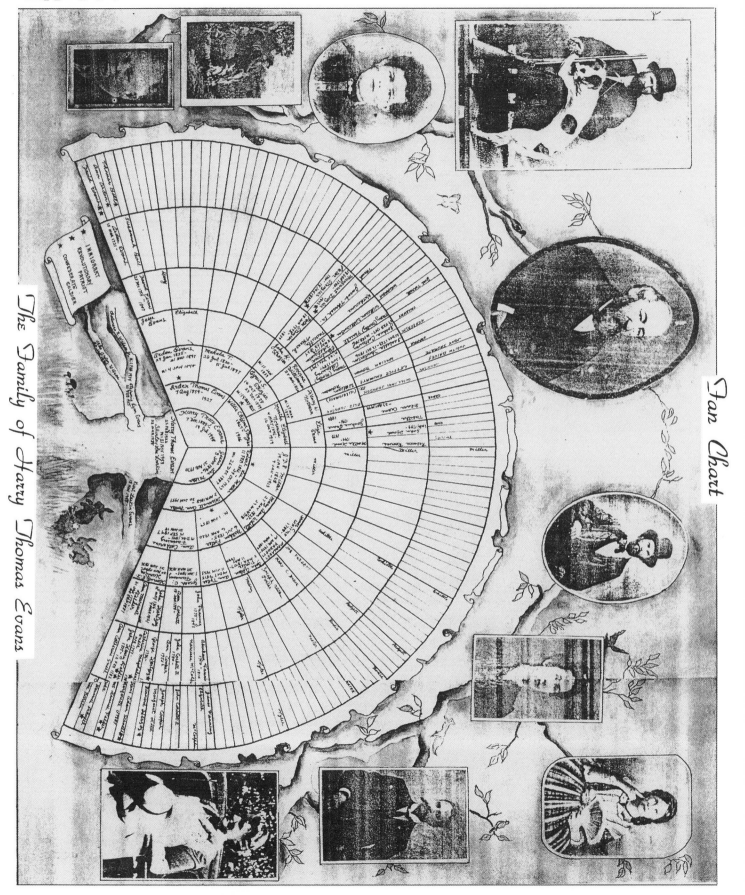

The Family of Harry Thomas Evans

Fan Chart

THE LADDER CHART. It may not be Jacob's Ladder, but it sure is heavenly when you can add another rung at the top! A neat way of showing genealogical links on the way back to that first identifiable ancestor in a particular blood line.

{V}

Augusta, Georgia

Dear Bette,

We've talked about all kinds of charts for the genealogist to use and today I have another one for you--a Ladder Chart. In Ancestoring I, the first journal published by the Augusta Genealogical Society, there is a perfect example. It was drawn up by one of our members, Harry Evans, to accompany a letter written to his first grandson, Jere, on the day Jere was born. Harry has said that I may share it with you. Please notice that this is a direct bloodline chart--neither all male lines nor all female lines--but the direct line back to Jere's oldest known Arden ancestor. Anyone can draw her own, it's easy. So try yours.

Beginning at the bottom of the "ladder," place your name, then to the left of that your husband's name (males always on the left, please) and his dates. On the second step of this ladder would go your mother's name and to the left (again), her husband, and so on, on up the ladder til you get to the earliest ancestor you can identify in that bloodline chart. Harry drew the Arden ladder for Jere since that was the baby's given name, but of course Jere has a whole "wardrobe" of ladder charts on his other lines that he can use when he gets old enough to enjoy genealogy.

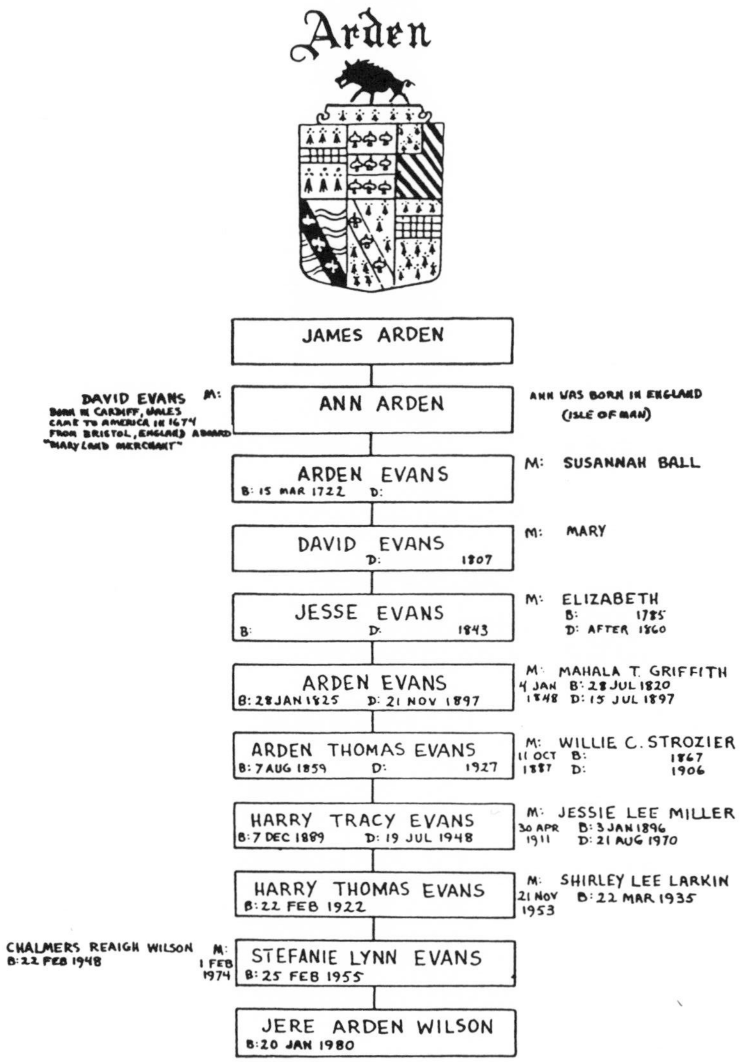

See how in Harry's chart there are three surnames involved to get back to the 11th generation? And see how Steffie's husband is shown on the left, and Harry's wife Shirley is shown on the right? And there it is, on one page, 11 generations!

Once these charts are completed, they can be framedand hung on the wall. And, if, like Harry, you can actually document a coat of arms--well, that's just the icing on the cake.

Well, dear, that's all the time I have today, there are skillions of leaves waiting for someone (me?) to rake them. My love to the family and hugs for all.

Love,

Vera

Chapter 3

Daily Mail: Incoming, Outgoing

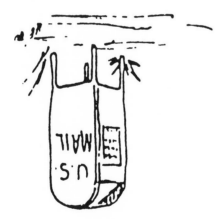
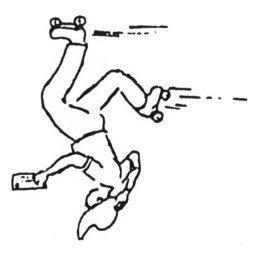

SASEs are a genealogist's research lifeline, but the lifethread is cut if they don't bring answers. Genealogical courtesy and these tips are guaranteed to produce more positive results.

ON PUTTING YOUR BEST "HAND" FORWARD. We all know about best foot forward, but it's equally important to put our best <u>hand</u> forward when we write genealogical query letters!

{V}

Augusta., Georgia

Dear Bette,

With summer just around the corner, all of us will be thinking about family research again, either by writing letters or doing it in our travels. I thought it a good time to remind you about the kind of letter you <u>should</u> write. I'm sure that you've received answers to the many queries you've placed in periodicals. Have you noticed that sometimes someone will enclose a photocopy of a letter written by someone in reply to a query? Remember <u>that</u> when <u>you</u> write letters!! If one of yours is passed on to someone else, well, was it one you were proud of?

It's easy to turn out a good letter if you follow a few simple rules. Always us a good black ribbon on your typewriter, or a black pen, so that your finished letter is legible. Many of us are getting older and our eyesight is failing--why should we strain our eyes trying to read a letter written on a faded ribbon (so, we don't!). Next, don't bore the reader with the life history of your ancestor (they could care less). Simply state the basic facts the reader will need to know in order to help you with your problem--straightforward and to the point. If you share the same families, always offer to exchange data with them as none of us ever has everything we need (or want) on a family. And ALWAYS proofread your letter before mailing!!

Another thing to remember is to steer clear of controversial subjects. You don't know the church the reader belongs to, or political leanings, and your comments may make your reader angry. Remember, this is a genealogical letter and should not include any subject that doesn't come under that heading.

Now for something new on the SASE. We've always stamped and addressed a #10 envelope for the reader to use when mailing material to us, but it had to be folded in thirds to fit <u>our</u> mailing envelope. This makes a rather bulky package which sometimes gets hung up in the machines at the post office and this could "mangle" the letter beyond recognition (and it ends up in File 13!). To make sure that this does not happen, the new system "we" have is to use a #9 envelope for our SASE and then put it in the #10 envelope we addressed to the person we are writing to for information (sneaky, huh?). Both sizes of envelopes are available at any office supply store.

Hon, did you notice anything after reading these simple rules (sure, you did!)? If you follow these guidelines in writing your letters, you have just written the type of letter that YOU LIKE TO RECEIVE!!! It was legible (no eye strain here); the problem area was listed briefly (no rambling through generations); it has an SASE enclosed for a reply; all "typos" have been corrected; it includes an offer to share, and offers a "thank you" for their help (they don't <u>have to</u>, you know!). All in all, a Grade A type of letter you would be proud for anyone to see.

Give my love to the family and write when you have time.

Love,
Vera

GENEALOGICAL COURTESY--THE GOLDEN RULE IN ACTION. Some reasons for using "good " manners: when requesting information by mail, or when researching in a public library.

{v}

Augusta, Georgia

Dear Bette,

I received a letter today that made me so angry that your next lesson is going to be on genealogical courtesy!!

This letter was from a lady who'd heard that I was searching the families of Lincoln County, Maine. She very bluntly said that she wanted me to send her everything I had on all the families. What nerve!

The first, and most important thing is to always send a SASE when writing for information from anyone. Even state-funded societies and archives and libraries like to get a SASE these days as tax money has to go for other more important things.

Next, never demand "everything" someone has. State the family you're looking for, the time period you're stuck in, and offer to pay for time spent in going through material (very few will charge for this), and if you want photocopies be sure to offer payment for those, too. THIS IS GENEALOGICAL GOOD MANNERS!! And always offer to share whatever you have with others, too.

While we're on this subject: A librarian is there to assist you in finding the books you need, not to research for you; she doesn't have the time. Don't damage the books by writing notes in the margins or underlining certain paragraphs. And never, ever, bend down the corners of a page; use a bookmark. Many of these books are out of print, very rare, and irreplaceable. If a page is turned down often enough, it eventually breaks off; imagine the frustration of tracing a family through the book and when you get to "your" page, it's half gone.

Also, don't write to some distant archives or town clerk with a foot-long list of things you want them to check for you. Write several times, with fewer requests in each letter, and keep each letter within the same time frame, such as three births covering the years 1876, 1877, 1878. This simplifies their jobs as old records were usually kept in huge ledgers.

What it really boils down to is, treat everyone and their possessions exactly the way you'd want yourself and your things treated: with care.

Say "Hi" to everyone for me and write soon.

Love,
Vera

{V}

Augusta, Georgia

Dear Bette,

I decided to write you a letter on how to write a letter (try slipping that sentence by your English teacher!). We're not talking about letters to friends or relatives, but about genealogical-query letters. Letters that you write asking for information, to an individual or an official, take a little more thought.

In writing to anyone, remember to send an SASE. Also keep the letter brief and to the point, especially when writing to a librarian or town clerk. They don't have the time to read about your complete problem, so tell them exactly how you hope they can help you. Tell them what you're looking for, names and dates, and ask if it's possible for them to check their records for you--you heard me--ASK. Don't put your request in the form of a command. "I want," "give me," these words should not be used, in fact, they aren't even polite. Always ask to be informed of the cost of any copies, and the postage, and offer to pay for their time. Not many will accept payment for their time, but by making the offer, you let them know that you understand their time is valuable. And remember that state libraries, archives, and societies are on budgets, too. Send them an SASE; postage is expensive and that's money they could use acquiring other records for us to check through.

When writing to someone with the same family surname as yours, it helps to send a brief outline of your ancestry. Or an ancestor chart. This lets them know how you fit into their line, if you do, and most will be pleased to hear from you, and to share with you (this works both ways, of course). Tell them where you're stuck and ask if they can help you. And always offer to help them with their problem generations if possible. You meet the nicest people this way!!

The main things to remember when writing these letters is to be courteous, brief, and never demanding. Write a letter that YOU would enjoy receiving, and want to answer. Because that's what you do want--someone to answer your letter. Write one that you wouldn't mind anyone reading, because you don't know who will see it. Many of us who want to share with others some data we've gotten through the mail just photocopy the letter and send it on; it's easier than retyping it (so be careful what you say).

That's all for today...write soon.

Love,
Vera

P.S. You do remember that SASE means "self-addressed, stamped envelope," I hope!

{V}

Augusta, Georgia

Dear Bette,

I have a new, great idea for you to try. It's something like the SASE that you send when writing letters to people you hope might be related to you. But this method almost assures you of a reply because it's easier for the other person.

At our genealogical society's "Following Footsteps is Fun" sessions, Glover Bailie conducts an excellent workshop called "Researching by Mail." In it, he stresses the importance of sending along a self-addressed stamped envelope when requesting help from someone. After one of his recent classes, Pat Colbert (all fired up to research, catching Glover's enthusiasm), decided to take his advice one step further. She asked friends going to (or through) towns where her ancestors originated, to photocopy phone book pages pertaining to her surnames in that area. Then Pat wrote to each person listed, briefly telling details of her search, and enclosed an addressed POSTCARD!! Typed on the back of each were the questions: Are you descended from this family? YES ____,   NO ____, and, Would you like to share data?   YES ____,   NO ____.

See how much easier a postcard is for a busy person on the receiving end--to just check YES or NO, then drop it in the mail. And, really, that's the only response you need at this stage of contact! Pat sent 18 cards, got back two "NO" and one "YES," and following up on the "YES," she took her line back five generations!

Isn't it nice that other "bugs" (like us) are willing to share great ideas like this??? Must run as dinner is late again (nothing new!).

Love,
Vera

{v}

Augusta, Georgia

Dear Bette,

As you've found out in doing research for yourself, we "genealogy nuts" are always on the lookout for a way to save money on the little things, in order to have enough to pursue our ancestors from their cradles to their graves. One expense that adds up quite fast is the cost of postage when writing letters asking for information from others. You use a 29¢ stamp to mail your letter, and another on the SASE included for the recipient to use for a reply. This amount to 58¢ for _each_ inquiry sent out by you (OUCH!). But there _is_ a way to save on postage when you're asking for just a bit of information (marriage/birth/ death dates, maiden name, or burial place, for instance).

In talking with Mrs. Fox, a very nice lady at our main post office, I mentioned this problem and wished there were some less expensive way to handle it. She suggested using a double postcard (I'd never heard of them!), and said that you buy them as a unit--one postcard attached to another postcard. The person you are requesting information from just writes an answer on the other postcard (the blank one, naturally!) and sends it back to you. She doesn't have to go searching through her desk for stationery, stamps, or anything. Very easy, huh? The best part, for the researcher, at least, is that the price of this unit is 38¢ (just the cost of two postcards). Using this method, you've saved 20¢ on each inquiry, but still got your questions off to the person you hoped had the answers you need.

If you think that going to the post office to get these cards is too much trouble, just to save 20¢, think again! I suggest that you make a list of all the _short_ letters you've written in the last six months, and then figure our how much you would have saved using double postcards. Using only ten of these double postcards saves you two dollars, and if you're like the rest of us, you've written ten time that many _notes_ in the last six months.

Well, dear, must get into the kitchen, so will close for now.

Love,
Vera.

{_V_}

Augusta, Georgia

Dear Bette,

Many times we've talked about how hard it is for most researchers to get to where the records are on their families--not all of us are free to travel all over the country. So in order to get the needed information we write hundreds of letters and send the required SASE--and <u>hope</u> to get answers. One problem, when dealing with an overworked staff of a library of archives, is that they <u>can't</u> <u>do</u> <u>it</u> now. For that reason they usually don't bother to answer if you seem impatient, and you are left wondering if they ever received your request--so you write again. Well, hon, there is a new way to get results--by letting the staff know you're aware of the problem and are willing to wait until they get time to answer you. It's called an SAP (what's so funny about a "nut" using a SAP!!??) and it usually gets results better than an SASE, especially when the recipient is short of time.

One of our AGS members, Becky Dozier, invented the SAP (self-addressed postcard!). Believing that her letters <u>had</u> been received by the various libraries, archives, town clerks, etc. and that they just didn't have time to answer <u>now</u>, she devised the SAP idea. Becky said that she puts her address on the front of the card and then divides the blank side into lines, each headed by a pertinent question about the record needed--all the clerk needs to do is check the right line and mail it.

Across the top of the card you'd put Fox County Probate Office, Re: Birth record of John Doe, b. 1862. Then the lines could be something like this: 1) <u>We have these records</u>--2) <u>We don't have them</u>-- 3) <u>May I buy copies?</u>--4) <u>When you have time can I expect a reply?</u> Be sure to give them the believed birthplace, or where land grant was, or where will was recorded--any data to make it easier for them. That's the secret--to make it easier for a busy clerk to help you.

Becky said that she had had fabulous results using this method. Almost all her postcards were returned, letting her know, 1) It had been received, 2) That the record existed, and 3) They would be glad to help as soon as they had time. The return of her SAP allowed her to work on other problem children without the nagging thought, "Did they get my request?"

Since family researchers are always looking for ways to find it easier for others to help us--don't you think this is a great idea! Try it, you'll like it.

Another storm coming up so must unplug everything (again!). Write when you have time and hugs to the family.

Love,

Vera

HE/WHO/ -- WHO/HE? Using pronouns in genealogical references is long on brevity and short on clarity.

{v}

Augusta, Georgia

Dear Bette,

Today's lesson is very short, and very "picky," and very important--especially if you want others to understand just what data you are looking for. The lesson is called the "he/who," "who/he" problem, and I'm sure you've noticed it before. I read a query recently that went this way:

John PRESTON, s/o Paul PRESTON & Alice WATERS, m. Dorothea GREYSTONE, d/o Stephen GREYSTONE & Virigina ELWOOD. He was b. ca. 1797 VA, need exact date & place.

Reading that last line, the first question is, WHO HE was b. ca. 1797!! John? Paul? Or father-in-law Stephen? They are all HE. The last line should read (if John is the one) John was b. 1797 VA. See how much difference that one distinction makes for the reader? Now it is clear which "he/who" the birthplace & date are needed for.

This problem isn't limited to queries. It's found in newspapers, biographies, and in any other printed material. It's simple to eliminate it. The writer needs to read the article, or query, as if it's the first time he, the writer, had seen it. If that were done, the writer would also ask the question, "he/who??"

Well, that's it! Told you it was going to be short, you should have believed me.

Love,
Vera

STATE + ZIP; BE SURE THEY'RE CORRECT. Don't try to outguess the post office--use the abbreviations <u>they</u> assign to the states if you really want your precious pleas to end up in the right hands.

{V}

Augusta, Georgia

Dear Bette,

Last month I wrote a "Help, Help!" letter to a lady in Arizona who is connected to one of my lines. Yesterday the post office returned it to me with "No such zip code in this state" written on it. I rambled through all my bits and pieces of paper looking for my list of postal abbreviations in order to prove that I was right (AR <u>did</u> stand for Arizona and that they were wrong) only to find that my logical conclusion was WRONG. Thinking that you might have the same problem, I'm sending you a list of ALL the two-letter state abbreviations now used by the United States Postal Serivce. Keep it handy!

AK--Alaska	MT--Montana
AL--Alabama	NE--Nebraska
AZ--Arizona	NV--Navada
AR--Arkansas	NH--New Hampshire
CA--California	NJ--New Jersey
CO--Colorado	NM--New Mexico
CT--Connecticut	NY--New York
DE--Delaware	NC--North Carolina
FL--Florida	ND--North Dakota
GA--Georgia	OH--Ohio
HI--Hawaii	OK--Oklahoma
ID--Idaho	OR--Oregon
IL--Illinois	PA--Pennsylvania
IN--Indiana	RI--Rhode Island
IA--Iowa	SC--South Carolina
KS--Kansas	SD--South Dakota
KY--Kentucky	TN--Tennessee
LA--Louisiana	TX--Texas
ME--Maine	UT--Utah
MD--Maryland	VT--Vermont
MA--Massachusetts	VA--Virginia
MI--Michigan	WA--Washington
MN--Minnesota	WV--West Virginia
MS--Mississippi	WI--Wisconsin
MO--Missouri	WY Wyoming

If you want to be sure your letters reach their destinations, it's extremely important that you choose the correct state abbreviation from the above list. Also, be sure to put the correct zip code (your local post office has a national directory) immediately after the state, or you take the chance of the having the automatic letter-sorting machine discard it. Sooner or later it <u>might</u> find its way back to you, but usually you're wondering why you didn't get an answer to your letter. So take a little extra care with addresses!

That's it for today--give the kids a hug for me, and write when you have time.

Love,
Vera

SIMPLIFY RESEARCH BY MAIL. Make it easy as possible for <u>them</u> to help <u>you</u> find that elusive ancestor--whether here or abroad.

{V}

Augusta, Georgia

Dear Bette,

Here it is--vacation time again! Most people think you work all year to pay the rent and put food on the table, but <u>we</u> know differently, don't we? We researchers know that we work all year in order to take research trips on our vacation time!! This year, I'm going to be content to stay home and research by mail. Of course, it isn't as easy as it used to be--many places have had budget cuts and are short on staff to answer mail or look up records for you. But they still try to help!

And we can help them, also. Your request usually has to wait until a personal check has cleared the bank and then your records are mailed to you. This ties up the staff in a way, as they have several requests pending at any given time. So let's do it another way--get the money to them in such a manner that it simplifies their jobs. For requests in the United States, consider sending a money order instead of your personal check. In fact, many places require money orders now.

But what about dealing with libraries or archives in a foreign country? Simple! If you are just asking for information or what they might have available, go to the post office and buy International Reply Coupons. Persons in another country use these at their post offices to pay for stamps of their country. If you know the record you're looking for is definitely there and you want to send money to cover cost of copies and return postage, then you have a choice of methods of sending money.

One is to buy an American Express Money Order. Another is to buy an International Money Order from the post office. Yet another is <u>really</u> simple: Just pick up your phone and dial toll-free 1-800-424-2923 and ask the folks at Ruesch International for a quote of current exchange rates with whatever country you are interested in. You mail your check to Ruesch to cover the amount you need in sterling, or whatever, plus a $2 overall service charge, and their check comes back in the sterling, or whatever, amount--which you mail off to the foreign address with your order. (Ruesch International, 1350 I St., NW, Washington, DC 20036.)

In all your requests, both here and overseas, the main thing is to make it as easy as possible for <u>them</u> to help you, because without them you wouldn't be able to chase those elusive ancestors all over creation--most genealogy nuts can't afford yearly trips to Canada or Europe or Great Britain--or a distant state!

Hope you are all well; my love to the family and write again.

Love,
Vera

{V}

Augusta, Georgia

Dear Bette,

Heard from a friend of mine today and she enclosed a letter you had written her asking for help on a family line. She said it wasn't clear just what you needed, but maybe I could help you. After crossing out half of your letter, I finally found what you were asking her for. Honey, you need some lessons in letter writing!! The people who get these letters are busy, and most won't bother with long, drawn-out problems, so you must learn to be brief and to the point. The beginning and the end are the same no matter to whom you're writing--you ask for info, then offer to pay for it, then include an SASE for a reply. The <u>body</u> of the letter is the important part, like so:

To a Town Clerk:
"I'm looking for the birth record of my great-grandfather John Doe, born in your city 3 Feb 1876, son of Thomas Doe and Alice Jones."

To a State Archives or Library:
"I've been told that you have indexed records of the pre-1810 settlers of Lincoln County. Would you have anything in your files on the MARSHALL family of St. George?"

A Query to a Genealogical Journal or Newsletter:
"Need parents & proof of birth for John DOE, b. 1827 Essex Co., MA, killed in battle in PA 1862, m. 1850 Essex Co. to Alice JONES, b. 1830 (MA?). They had 7 ch., including my grandfather, Thomas, b. 1853 Essex Co., d. 1897 Hartford, CT, m. 15 Jun 1878 to Juanita SMITH at Hartford. Will exch. info on Thomas & his siblings."

To Answer a Query:
"I'm also descended from the DOE family of Massachusetts, and have enclosed data pertinent to your John Doe's parents. Have also enclosed my family group sheet so you can see how we are related, and to ask if you have any information on my branch of the family."

To Answer A Query:
"Saw your query and thought you might be able to use the enclosed data on John Doe of Essex County, Massachusetts, which I found while checking records for my branch of the DOE family."

Do you get the point? Each one is complete in itself--no extra data included which might cloud the issue. You've stated what you need, and in the briefest way possible. <u>This</u> type of letter gets read, and answered--the others usually end up in the waste basket. Try it next time.

Love,
Vera

WHEN THE THERMOMETER HITS 100°, THINK QUERIES! Assuming you're not an English-man or a mad dog*, spend these hot days in air conditioned comfort organizing your files, and then send off queries seeking help from other researchers.

{V}

Augusta, Georgia

Dear Bette,

With temperatures around the country hitting the 100 degree or over mark (mostly over!), it has certainly changed the plans of many researchers. Most of us use our summer vacation time to chase down as many ancestors as possible, but who in their right minds (WE ARE!!) would go running through cemeteries, etc. in this heat??

Now is a good time to settle down in your air conditioned house and go through all the family data already collected. Usually, when we do this, we find that there is a lot of material in our files that we'd forgotten was there, and possibly we are still wasting time looking for something we already have. Take out one family surname at a time and separate it into generations--grouping parents and children together. Then get out your blank charts and enter all names, dates, and places for each person, being sure to enter in ink only proven data. Unproven information can be entered in pencil which can be erased later when you find the facts to bear out your assumption, such as a definite marriage date instead of "m ca.1822." Be sure you have, and list, the documentation for each claimed name or date.

Once you have all your information listed on the proper charts in the proper manner, you are then ready for the next step in your research, the most important step if you are to continue collecting data to prove your line. Take a notebook and begin by listing _every_ piece of information that you still need. Aunt Jane married about 1820--you need a definite date. Grandparents married in New York 22 Feb 1876 --you need the town or county. Your other grandfather, according to the census you have, was born 1860-1870 in Maine--you need to pin down the exact year of birth and the town where he was born. Get the idea? When you finish listing the things still needed, you'll feel as if you <u>don't</u> <u>know</u> more than you <u>know</u>! That's half the fun of doing genealogy, always wondering, "Where is it?", "Will I ever find it?"

Okay, you have your list of "Don't Haves." What do you do now? If you aren't able to set up another research trip right now, you do have another choice, a choice that we family researchers would be totally lost without--QUERIES. Sort out your needed data by location and start typing queries to be sent to periodicals, etc., in that area. The more queries you send out, the better chance of them being seen by others researching the same families. Don't be discouraged if you hear nothing for months (or even years) --that query is out there in some library's holdings and sooner or later it <u>will</u> be seen by other searchers. Those of us who live a great distance from our research area probably receive more help from people who answer our queries than we do from any other source. "They" usually know of others looking for the same lines and gladly share with you. It's like a circle, what assistance you may give a querier comes back to you in the future from another one. And that's one of the "perks" of this family research business-- everyone helps everyone else.

Well, must run. Many things to do outside before it gets hot out there. Write when you have time, and give my love to the family.

Love,
Vera

---

*"Mad dogs and Englishmen go out in the mid-day sun."--Noel Coward

NO ANSWER TO YOUR QUERIES? Sometimes when we send a query to a genealogical publication and receive no answer, we can't understand why. Surely someone in that vicinity knows something about our ancestor. Here's light on why some of us hear nothing from our queries.

{V}

Augusta, Georgia

Dear Bette,

What are queries? Well, they are a form of advertisement, and are an invaluable aid to genealogists who are unable to travel to each locale where their ancestors lived. When you've come up against a blank wall, place a query in a genealogical publication, making sure that you include not only the data you need but enough information to <u>really</u> identify the person in question (there may be several men with the same name). Also, when you make contact with others working on the same lines, you can all share your material. There are good queries, and bad ones. Let's discuss the bad ones first.

There's "Naive Nellie." She says, "George Jones married Jane Moore, need marriage date and all their children." Now, Nellie won't get any answers from this. The reader doesn't know <u>when</u> George lived, <u>where</u> he lived (or even IF he lived), so why look through the files.

Then we have "Greedy Gus." He says, "Want ancestry and <u>all</u> descendants of John Gibson. I think he lived in Vermont in the 1800s." Gus doesn't want much--just everything--on a man who might have lived in a certain state during a 100-year period. No answers for him either.

Get the idea? Now let me show you how to write one that should bring results. You have to remember that the reader is a stranger and will know only what you tell him. A well-worded query contains at least 4 things: <u>what</u> you need, <u>who</u> was involved, and <u>when</u> and <u>where</u> the event occurred. For example:

> Need date of marriage of George Lamb, b. 1737 at Malden, Mass.
> son of John and Sara (Hasty) Lamb. He m. Mary Stevens, b. 1743
> at Boston, Mass., dau of William and Hannah (Andrews) Stevens.
> Their first child, John, was bpt June 1763 in the First Church
> of Boston. George's will was probated 27 July 1794 at
> Billerica, Mass. Will refund postage. (Then your name and
> address.)

This query immediately separates George Lamb from any others who may have existed. It tells the reader three possible towns where the marriage might have taken place, AND, it gives a time span. Few girls married before age 15, so the marriage took place after 1758 (when Mary turned 15), and before June 1763 (when first child was baptized). All readers who have an ancestor named George Lamb who would fit into the framework that you have given them, will check their files to see if they have what you need. And, if you're lucky, one of them will!!

It goes without saying that <u>every</u> reply to your query should be answered with a "Thank you," and the promised postage sent. If you want more information from anyone, always include a self-addressed, stamped envelope (SASE to genealogists).

Well, dear, the lesson is over for today (never thought you'd go back to school, did you?). Hope this helps you get some results. Write soon.

Love,
Vera

"KEEP PUTTING THEM OUT THERE!" Advertising your research needs pays off, even though answers to published Queries may be weeks, months, or even years in coming.

{v}

Augusta, Georgia

Dear Bette,

It was great to get your letter and hear the news of the "Western" branch of the family; love to be brought up-to-date on all the new arrivals. But the rest of your letter was terrible--so many complaints, you poor thing. But don't cry on _my_ shoulder. I've BEEN THERE! And it's not like you're telling it. So-- you placed a _few_ queries in a couple of magazines and didn't get any answers! So what? Keep putting them out there! In this research game, the law of averages says that you usually help more people than you get answers from. Only a beginner would want results "yesterday," the rest of us have already found out that you might get an answer in weeks, months, or even years. You just keep pushing your problem children any time the chance arises.

A friend, Betsey McCloskey, placed several "maiden names needed for some ALBEE wives" queries about six years ago. Not one person wrote her. Last year, a lady wrote giving the information she needed and more. The lady had just started her research and had gone to the library and looked through a lot of publications from genealogical and historical societies around the country, and there were Betsey's queries--just waiting for someone to find them.

You can see that the results aren't immediate when a query is placed in a magazine, so don't get discouraged. Get stubborn and put more out there. Where do you put them? That's easy. All states have historical societies; within the state you have societies on a city, county, or area level. There are many genealogical societies in every part of the country, and then there are groups that put out newsletters or journals with query sections and early records of their area. Most of these give free queries to anyone who joins their society or subscribes to their newsletter. But there are other groups that publish newsletters, groups that don't require you to join or buy their publication before using your query--instead, they will publish a query for a small fee (so much per word, etc.). Some will even accept a free query from a non-member if they have the space to do so (will not eliminate a member's query for a non-member's).

With all these sources available in which to place your queries it would be crazy not to take advantage of them. And anyone who is a member of a society and doesn't use this service is losing a chance to maybe clear up a problem line. You don't have to limit your queries to just the area the publication covers. These newsletters are exchanged with others around the country, and somewhere, sometime, someone will see your query. Remember that people moved all over the place years ago. Some from the South now have descendants in Canada (or anywhere); those from New England have descendants out West. You don't know exactly where others, descended from your ancestor, are living now (look where _you_ got to). So place queries in every publication that will allow it, AND be sure to answer every query you see when YOU have information that will help someone else. This last bit is very important. Each time you help someone you can tell them about your problem, and that's one more person who knows who you are looking for!!

Well, dear, guess I'd better quit yelling at you. Dinner due in an hour and the stove is still cold, so must get in the kitchen or _I'll_ be in the dog house. Write soon.

Love,
Vera

{V}

Augusta. Georgia

Dear Bette,

It's funny that you should be asking me the same question that many others have been asking over the last several months: "What happens to all the self-addressed stamped envelopes that I send out with my requests for information letters??" I'm sorry that I can't answer your question with any degree of definite knowledge--have often pondered about it myself. To answer a letter when the person has furnished the SASE is very simple (isn't it?). The recipient has two choices here. He can send the data you asked for, using your SASE, or he can take your letter and write, "I'm sorry but don't have the information you need," and, again, return it to you using your SASE. Each is an easy and courteous way to deal with the situation. A serious researcher will answer all letters of inquiry that he gets, even those without the SASE, because we know how it feels to not have someone reply to your questions--and because we have learned that to be courteous to others is one of the most important things in doing research.

So, back to your question. What <u>does</u> happen to them? Did your letter get lost in the mail? Get delivered to the wrong address? Did your stamp come unglued? Did the people you sent it to bother to open it? Read it? Questions that never get answered because you never get an answer.

Another thought we have is, did he cover your address on the envelope with a self-stick label and put his address on it and use it for his own purposes? Or maybe what he really wants is the stamp--a friend of mine wrote an archives for information on one of her ancestors, sending the required fee and an SASE--they took the fee, sent her the data she wanted, AND returned her SASE to her WITH THE STAMP NEATLY CUT OUT OF THE CORNER! Believe it, I saw it!!

Even though we all have questions such as those above concerning our stamped envelopes none of us would consider altering the traditional method of trying to obtain information by mail. With today's high postal rates, it's about the only way you can assure yourself of getting a reply. True, many people don't answer your query but many others will answer simply because you included an SASE.

One friend said she had over 75 letters "floating around out there," all with an SASE in them, and if she just knew where "they" had buried them she'd go get them. She was very discouraged, and rightly so, because she replies to every query she gets. But she still includes one in every query letter she sends out--and you do the same!

What it really means is that you treat other researchers in the manner that you wish to be treated. Always use that SASE for the purpose it was meant for--an answer. It is as important for us to know our letter reached its destination as it is to get answers to our queries. If it reached you and you wrote that you couldn't help--that's one source of data we can cross off our list. Otherwise we're left dangling in mid-air, wondering whether to try again--or--or--

Well dear, enough for today, must get outside and play (play??). My love to all and write again soon.

Love,
Vera

{V}

Augusta, Georgia

Dear Bette,

I've been meaning to write a long letter but have been so busy that time slips on by me. Did you ever get the feeling that the longer you live, the faster time goes? Ah, yes!! Anyway, I had a great idea for you--although it's borrowed from a friend of mine.

Last Christmas, we received several cards with ancestor charts included with them. Did you ever think what you could accomplish doing this? Just imagine getting holiday cards or letters off to 50 friends and family members with the enclosed ancestor chart which shows them where your problem areas are!

The chart also lets relatives see how their families followed through each generation. Some of them may have never realized who their immediate ancestors were, or how they are connected to the various branches of the family tree.

Anyway, my charts are being readied for the holiday season and you should do the same. Someone out there may have just the bit of information you need! Don't you think this IS a great idea? (Of course, you do!)

Write when you can and give my love to the family.

Love,
Vera

KEEPING A CORRESPONDENCE RECORD. An easy way to keep track of all those search letters, and eliminate the possibility of (horrors!) asking the same person for the same information twice.

{V}

Augusta, Georgia

Dear Bette,

How do I know "Who I asked what?" Well, I now make carbon copies of all letters written, but in the beginning, I made a chart somewhat like the one I sent you--the one for keeping a record of your research. You just have to change the headings. Like this:

```
---------------------------------------------------------------------------------
Date sent ¦ To    ¦Subject ¦ Info needed ¦ Answer Rec'd ¦ Info Rec'd
---------------------------------------------------------------------------------
2 Feb 1983 George  Alex    birthdate    15 Feb 1983    b. 1786 *
           Jones   Smith                               Boston, MA


---------------------------------------------------------------------------------
                        * = proof sent   # = no proof sent
```

To go with this chart, and my research chart, I have a genealogical address book. Each person, archives, library, state or town officers, and all publications that I've placed a query in, are listed in this book. There are no family or personal friends listed; it's strictly genealogy. And, beside each name I've written the "family" connection, so all you have to do is look under "Jones" and everything is there: name, address, and "the Smith family." If you're more comfortable with 3x5 cards, maybe they would work better for you than keeping all the addresses in a book.

All this may sound complicated, but just make believe you're doing office work again. Remember--files, cross-files, sub-files, etc., etc., etc. (some fun!).

Love,

Vera

ON JOINING YOUR "BACK HOME" SOCIETY. Lots of happy surprises may await you when you join the genealogical society back where your ancestors called "home."

{v}

Augusta, Georgia

Dear Bette,

This time I've got a question for you (the worm turns, etc.). Ages ago, you said that you were considering joining the genealogical society in New York where most of your families are located. Have you done it yet?? If not, then do it NOW!!

Most of us get so interested in the research that we don't stop to think of how the records became available to us. Well, I'll tell you: they are likely transcribed or photocopied by a group of people in that area who wanted to preserve all old records--a genealogical society. And it's important that we, the researchers at a distance, give them the support they need to continue their work. That means joining their society and, with our dues, giving them a little more incentive to "keep up the good work." There are societies in almost any area of the country, you just have to seek them out. Also, we benefit from all their work by getting information from them about our families, and being able to send in free queries. A few examples for you. . .

Dee Mitchell, an AGS member, decided after much searching that her ancestor (one she had completely lost) should be in the area near Lorain County, Ohio. She joined the Lorain County Genealogical Society and in her application mentioned that she was trying to find this ancestor. Imagine her surprise when a letter arrived from the editor saying he'd checked one of their cemetery books for this man and then enclosed the record of his burial. Dee also joined the Connecticut Society of Genealogists and through them found a third cousin who has given her LOADS of family material. Suppose she had not joined these societies (I can't bear to think of that, and neither can she)--her great-great grandfather would still be missing!

I long ago joined the St. George, Maine Historical Society. In the beginning, it was only to have contacts in the area where my Marshalls began, but one of the founders of the society, Steve Sullivan, changed all that. He sent me the parents and siblings of my "lost" ancestor, and went one better by telling me where I could find it in print at the Maine State Library. Suppose I hadn't joined???

Another reason for joining a "back home" society was given recently by a new member of AGS, Thelma Paschal, of California. She said that she had many ancestors who originated in this area and wanted to join our society "to show my support of all the good things you're doing." Wasn't that a lovely thought!!

You can see from this that help is given AND received, which is the foundation of family research. Our dues help them to copy more records (church, cemetery, etc.) and their ability to copy more records helps US find more ancestors. So get out the checkbook and join one in your area now (or two, or maybe three) and show your support of the hard work they are doing in order to preserve old records.

Must run, so I'll close for now. Hope to hear from you soon. My love to the family.

Love,
Vera

P.S.: If you don't know the name of a genealogical society in your area of research, find a copy of Mary K. Meyer's <u>Meyer's</u> <u>Directory</u> <u>of</u> <u>Genealogical</u> <u>Societies</u> <u>in</u> <u>the</u> <u>USA</u> <u>and</u> <u>Canada</u>.

Chapter 4

You _Can_ Go Home Again!

Research trips are icing on the cake for "ancestorin'" devotees. They can walk on their ancestor's home turf, and click a time machine to put themselves there, as it was "back then."

PREPARING FOR VACATION RESEARCH TRIPS. Time spent ahead planning for summer research trips pays big dividends. . .and doubles the fun!

{V}   Augusta, Georgia

Dear Bette,

I could see from your letter that you're on Cloud Nine (not that I wouldn't be, too!). A two-month vacation just to do research in the East is better than a trip to Europe!! But, since this is your first time, you must plan ahead on what you need to do, and where it needs doing, so that nothing is overlooked at each stop. So, get our your ahnentafel (you <u>did</u> make one, didn't you?) and this is your beginning. The table is a complete listing of your direct lines, all the data you can prove, and all that you can't, and the "can't" is where work is needed. Then, make a list for each ancestor and what information is needed to complete that line. Add to that, the source where you think the data may be found--archives, state library, courthouse, land office, genealogical or historical society, etc.

Then, write letters to each place asking what their open hours are. Many places are staffed by volunteers and, therefore, are open at odd hours instead of the usual "nine to five." It would be a shame to get there only to find them closed. One important item to remember is that most of these places have rules as to what you can take inside the building, such as notebooks, pencils, and file folders, BUT no purse or carryall. Believe it or not, many irreplaceable items have "walked" out of libraries in someone's purse. So ask about their rules when you write.

Another item of importance to take along is a "census heading sheet." You'll need to know exactly <u>what</u> every census covered, so, beginning with 1790 and going as far as needed to cover your research time period, lay the census forms down, one on top of the next, covering all except the <u>column headings</u>--then photocopy it. The finished copy will show what info was asked for by that year's census taker--all on one sheet. That's easier than trying to figure everything out <u>after</u> you get into the censuses.

Another thing to remember is to document everything: book title and author, vital records page number, the file number if found on a microfilm record, and <u>always</u> record WHERE the record was located (which archives, which library, etc.). Keep a list of every place you searched and every record you found there. If unsuccessful, it's just as important to note that NOTHING WAS FOUND. If you don't keep such a record ("searched 1830 census Marlboro, Massachusetts and Joe Doe not listed that year"), some-time in the future you will search that census again, thinking that it was one source overlooked by you earlier (I've done it many times!).

Now, you're all set, the letters written, the rules and open hours of the libraries are known, you have your ahnentafels, your census heading sheets, your file folders, plenty of sharpened pencils and a small sharpener, notebooks (I prefer the looseleaf type), and change for the copy machines. Your change and smaller items can be conveniently carried in a small, 3-ring zippered plastic "pocket" that fits into your looseleaf binder--you can find them at any school supply counter. Look out, libraries, here she comes!!

Since you have a nice long vacation, you might want to go beyond the library circuit when you get back to your ancestor's turf. I heard of a new wrinkle in "vacation searching" tried last summer by a man in Tennessee. For a graduation present, he took his daughter on a tour through several states, just the two of them, visiting homesites, cemeteries, etc. where their ancestors once lived. He armed himself with a Polaroid camera and a nice, big album equipped with plastic envelopes to slip the pictures into. By the end of the trip, he had a beautiful memory book of photos taken along the way, of his daughter at her great-grandfather's grave, of him in front of an old homestead, etc., etc. The album was an "instant" creation each day as they went along--and a priceless memory book for the future for <u>both</u> generations! So, pack your bags, load the car, head East, and above all, HAVE FUN!

Love,
Vera

ANCESTOR-HUNTING WITH A CAMERA. Stalking ancestors through deeds and wills has long been a big deal with genealogical detectives. Now more and more are using cameras--and building a visual family history.

{V}

Augusta, Georgia

Dear Bette,

Did you ever think that vacations and weekend trips could be used for another reason besides "just having fun?" A few of our AGS members have used their spare time to locate their ancestors' old homes and burial places, and to record them on film for more lasting memories. Wish I'd thought of that years ago!

Remember that I told you recently about one member, Tim Sloan, who decided to take his daughter back to the area where his ancestors lived, and, in order to have a permanent record of the trip, he packed camera, film, and photo albums. At each town, house, or cemetery, he explained to her who these people were and how they related to the family. Then the photos were taken and immediately placed in the albums. By the time the trip was over, the albums were filled--and she had received a crash course in ancestor hunting.

Another member, George Christenberry, in June went to Alabama on a similar trek. He made photos of homes and gravesites of his ancestors, and was especially thrilled to find the cemetery where his great-grandfather is buried. He took lots of pictures there. There was still some film in his camera when he returned home, the day before graduation ceremonies at Augusta College. As recently retired president of the college, he had the honor of presenting his granddaughter with her diploma, so he asked his wife to take lots of pictures of her, in cap and gown, during the ceremony. The biggest thrill came when the pictures were developed. One of them showed his granddaughter standing beside the grave of her great-great-great-grandfather. Here was a mystery! He hadn't taken a picture like that--in fact, his grand-daughter wasn't even with him in Alabama! Then they realized that it was a double exposure, totally unplanned, but a wonderful keepsake for his granddaughter. Can't you see her face 50 years from now, dragging out that album and telling HER grandchildren all about the day she graduated, and how her great-great-great-grandfather was there when she did!

Dr. Christenberry is really "bitten by the bug." Last month, he went to Lenoir, North Carolina to seek out "whatever" on the Shells and Earnhardts. He came across a stained glass window dedicated to the memory of his great-grandfather, in the church the family had attended there (of course, he took a picture!). Wasn't that great luck to find the window? Though he's new to genealogy, he had made some fantastic discoveries, and, needless to say, he is "hooked," although he may not quite realize it yet (all of "us" know, though, don't we?). From now on, he will live and breathe to find the next piece of this great puzzle we call ancestor hunting.

Honey, you know that a family researcher wouldn't dream of leaving the courthouse without a photocopy of the will, or the deed, (or an arrest) that we found there, and this way we build a visual history of our ancestors' lives. Using the camera to record churches and schools attended, the homes lived in, and cemeteries they were buried in--isn't this just another way to continue a "visual history?" We have always used a camera to take pictures of the family, and, in this way, we record memories for the future. Now we know that the camera can also be used to record and build memories of the past. So be sure to stock up on plenty of film before starting out on your next vacation trip! And you might even think to plan some double exposures!

My love to everyone, and write soon.

Love,
Vera

{*V*}

Augusta, Georgia

Dear Bette,

Your letter caught me in the middle of cooking and baking "goodies" for James (am a <u>firm</u> believer in the old maxim, "the way to a man's heart is through his stomach"). You said that you two were combining a vacation and a research trip again this year. It sounds like loads of fun, but I want to remind you of some advice given to you before. Always (!) write ahead of time to the places you wish to visit!!!

Due to budget cuts, many libraries and state archives have had to curtail their service to the public, for instance. The form this takes is, usually, closing the doors at least one day each week--the South Carolina Archives is closed on Mondays at present, as are others. The GA Archives offers another kind of problem due to budget cuts: Original documents are pulled only twice a day, at 10 a.m. and 1:30-2:30 p.m. It would be awful to travel several hundred miles to do research, only to find you can't get in--or cannot have ready access to what you came for in the first place! It's much easier to write or phone first, asking when they are open, or what other research restrictions are, then plan your itinerary accordingly. To help you get off to a good start on your new research habit, the Georgia Archives phone number is 404/656-2393.

Also, check with historical or genealogical societies ahead of time. Their library staffs are usually made up of volunteers, therefore, they open only on those days when a volunteer staff is available. Our AGS library is open on Sunday, Monday, Wednesday, and Saturday and is closed during certain holiday periods. It is run by a lovely group of dedicated librarians of the day who give of their time on days off from work, school, retirement activities, etc. Think how disappointed you'd be if, not knowing our open days, you arrived on Tuesday, all geared up to do research, and found only a locked door in front of you! Or, if you found professionally staffed archives which would be open every day normally, temporarily closed--perhaps for asbestos removal or relocation of its collection. Several state archives are in the asbestos-removal phase these days, and some are closed for weeks or months at a time!

So, dear, write first, and nothing will mar your vacation. Write soon and give my love to all the family.

Love,
Vera

PLANNING FAMILY RESEARCH ON YOUR VACATION? Cemeteries and courthouses are great, but don't forget other places to look for your ancestors as you plan that vacation itinerary!

{V}
Augusta, Georgia

Dear Bette,

Now that summer has finally arrived, everyone seems to have planned a little family research to coincide with their vacations. There are courthouses, churches, and cemeteries to start with, but don't forget other places to look for your ancestors, like libraries and records of patriotic and fraternal organizations, and in other repositories along your route--museums, church archives, etc.

We've talked before about the Daughters of the American Revolution, which has a wonderful library in Washington, DC, but there are many others, such as Colonial Dames of America, Colonial Dames of the XVII Century, United Spanish War Veterans, Society of the Cincinnati, United Daughters of the Confederacy, War of 1812 Society, etc. This list could go on and on if space permitted, but the main thing to remember about these societies is that they have records on their members, past and present, proving the member's lineage back to a remote ancestor (perhaps you can connect into one of these lines!), and most societies maintain very fine libraries which we may use for a small fee if not a member.

Then we have fraternal organizations such as Woodmen of the World, Masons, Knights of Pythias, Knights of Columbus, Benevolent and Protective Order of Elks, the Improved Order of Red Men, etc. Fraternal organizations are of particular interest to a family researcher. Many times you have seen on gravestones the emblem of one of these groups. . .right? What you may not know is that many of these organizations pay old-age benefits to their members, maintain homes for the aged, poor, and for widows and orphans of their members. Can't you just imagine the records that are kept?? If you know, or just hope, that an ancestor was a member of a fraternal or patriotic organization, then this is a source you can't afford to overlook (it also gives you another reason to be more aware of these emblems on tombstones!). Your public library can give you addresses of national or state headquarters of these organizations, and a letter might bring you just the bit of information you need, such as available research opportunities in the area you're visiting.

As for other depositories you might not think of checking on: Local museums just may have old Bibles, journals, or area maps! Also, what with the crunch for space in courthouses these days, museums have accepted custody of old courthouse records in many communities. Wouldn't <u>that</u> be a bonanza for you? Historical and genealogical societies may house local genealogists' collections. The Camden (SC) Archives houses a wonderful DAR collection, for instance.

Another "other" is church record repositories. Here in Georgia, the Baptist Archives at Stetson Library on campus at Mercer University in Macon, is very helpful. In South Carolina, Furman University in Greenville has Baptist records and Wofford College in Spartanburg has Methodist ones. In Alabama, Samford University Library has great Baptist records and Historical Foundation of the Presbyterian and Reformed Churches at Montreat, North Carolina, has an excellent collection of church minutes, etc. from all over the South. In Texas, Austin is a double jackpot. The national archives of the Episcopal Church is located on the campus of the Episcopal Seminary of the Southwest, and the Texas State Catholic Archives is located in the city, also. The William Perkins Library at Duke University has many old Methodist records, and Guilford College in Guilford, North Carolina has superb Quaker records. In fact, you might want to check in at colleges all along your route to find what their Special Collections hold--even the smallest of small colleges usually has an interesting local history collection and who knows, they just might have cemetery surveys or other pertinent genealogical material not held elsewhere.

Well, dear, all for now. Have fun planning for all those "other" places you'll visit.

Love,
Vera

{**V**}

Augusta, Georgia

Dear Bette,

Forgot to mention something else you need to take on your research trip--a simple coding system.
If you try to write down everything in detail in your research "finds," from beginning to end, by the time
you get home your fingers will be worn down to stubs! So, make a list of common abbreviations to take
with you and tape them in the front of your notebook so you can check quickly if you need to.

First, to show relationship, you have the "ofs" (/o)--daughter (d/o), son (s/o), husband (h/o),
parents (par/o). . .get the idea? Next you have "records." Cem. (cemetery, of course!), T. (Town), V.
(Vital), Chh. (Church), L. (Land), Prob. (Probate), etc.--always followed by Rec. (Records). Ve-r-r-r-y
simple, huh? But you would be surprised how much time it can save you if you learn to use these
abbreviations consistently.

Then you have locations where the records were found: Library (Lib), Archives (Ar), Courthouse
(C.H.), etc. If you're searching several states, use the two-digit letters the Post Office uses, FL for Florida,
etc. Now isn't that easier? And the more you use the system, the sooner it will become second nature to do
it that way.

When you return from your trip, you'll be able to type a translation of "bur/o John Doe & w/Jane
Smith, p. 72, Meriden Cem. Rec., B.C.-CT St Lib, Htfd" into:

"Burial records of John Doe & wife Jane Smith, <u>Meriden, Connect-</u>
<u>icut</u> <u>Cemetery</u> <u>Records</u>, p. 72, located in Barbour Collection,
State Library, Hartford, Connecticut"

as documentation for your records.

Your fingers will not be stubs, and you'll have saved yourself so much time you had extra
research hours to dig deeper and deeper for those elusive clues our ancestors left so well-hidden!

Must run--the lawnmower is waiting. Have fun, then tell me all about it!

Love,
Vera

ON "MORE NEW THINGS UNDER THE SUN." There's a Sherlock Holmes gene (known to most folks as a "curiosity bump"), which helps us find the absolute <u>easiest</u> way to get our research act together. This tip is tuned to your vacation research trips.

{V}

Augusta, Georgia

Dear Bette,

You know how I'm always telling you, "Genealogy is fun!" and you always say, "Yeah??" or "Sometimes." Well, I'm going to prove it--researching IS fun!! Or funny!

Last week, my friend Carrie was telling me that her brother and new bride wanted to know what there was of interest in the states they would travel through on their honeymoon. So she decided to call the states of interest for available brochures for them. The first state called gave her a toll-free number, this was for the tourist bureau covering the entire state of North Carolina; the number was 1-800-VISITNC. Don't you just love that!! And easy to remember, too. The next step, of course, was to wonder if all states had this service for travelers, and, wondering, we <u>had</u> to know (curiosity, that's common to all genealogists!).

I dug around in my library and found <u>American Information Handbook</u>, by Orville V. Webster, III, and it had a section on tourism offices for all states. We found that some states had 800 numbers like: 225TRIP for Kentucky, BUCKEYE for Ohio, VISITPA for Pennsyvlvania, and VISITGA for Georgia, ESCAPES for Wisconsin, and 33GUMBO for Louisiana. The one that really tickled our senses of humor was the Chattanooga, Tennessee number, TRACK29 (remember that old song "Chattanooga Choo Choo?).

Naturally, we couldn't leave things there, so we decided to try and figure out if the numbers for other states "said something." We took the telephone number given and compared it to the letters given on the telephone dial, and--BINGO! Wyoming's number was 1-800-225-5996--that works out to CALLWYO, and New York State's number was 1-800-225-5697, which works out to CALLNYS. Then came West Virginia's CALLWVA, and <u>my</u> favorite, Michigan's 5432YES.

There's only one thing more fun than planning a family research trip, and that is combining it with a visit to historic places in the area where the family lived. That also is part of your family's history. So, next time you decide to make a trip to "dig up old bones," first call a toll-free number like those above and find out what else is available for you to see while in that area.

Well, dear, James and the cat went to bed ages ago, and that's where I'm headed. Give hugs to all for me and write soon.

Love,
Vera

Chapter 5

Names and Other Family Foibles

Things every famiy has in common. Names and
Foibles. The smart genealogist knows that the
first has multitudinous spellings and the second,
only God knows.

{V}

Augusta, Georgia

Dear Bette,

This will be a short letter as I'm ready for some shut-eye. I found something funny and wanted to share it with you (as one nut to another?) You're aware by now that we family researchers sometimes get very smug about our ancestors, and lose our senses of humor along the way. Then something comes along to restore it, and we're off and running again. . .this article restored mine!

I was browsing through an early Southern Echoes, the AGS newsletter, and saw an article entitled "Who Says Genealogy Isn't Fun?" Well, that hit my eye because, of course it's fun, everyone knows it's fun (don't they?), and if it isn't fun why do we spend so much time doing it?? If you'd like to read the entire article, go by your library and get the February 1985 issue. But here is what sent me off into gales of laughter. It said:

"To understand the four nationalities that make up the United Kingdom, we must recognize that:

SCOTS: Keep the Sabbath and everything else they can get their hands on.

IRISH: Don't believe in anything and will fight like hell to defend it.

WELSH: Pray on their knees and everybody else.

ENGLISH: Feel like they were born to rule the world and relieve the Almighty of any responsibility.

Isn't that hilarious!! It gets your nose out of the air and your feet back on solid ground, and is especially funny if, like us, all your ancestors fall into these four groups (my sides still hurt!). Isn't it great to laugh at yourself!!

Well, dear, that's all for tonight, must get my beauty (?) sleep. Write soon.

Love,
Vera

LOGIC VERSUS EMOTION. Logic would have you include rascals on your family tree when you write your family's history, but emotion can make it difficult to include them!

{V}

Augusta, Georgia

Dear Bette,

It was great to hear from you again. It had been so long that I thought you'd left the country or something. Instead, you've been enjoying that honeymoon you didn't get all those years ago. Glad you had a wonderful time. And I'm glad you have a few questions for me, too. Tonight, we'll talk about logic versus emotion in doing family research, okay?

Everyone will tell you that I'm crazy to say that there's no place for emotion when you're tracing your ancestors, but I stand firm; emotions get in the way! I think we all agree that a family history should be an accurate account of the people and events in your ancestry. But some find it hard to include in their "history" all the rogues or less-than-perfect ancestors they dig up. That's emotion getting in the way--all their ancestors had to be above reproach. They get so wrapped up in the "General" or the "Governor" or "The Reverend" in their lines that they forget one important thing: ANCESTORS WERE HUMAN! And humans aren't infallible; they make mistakes, bad judgments, all kinds of things. They're good, and bad, and some in between. Every aristocratic family had its "black sheep," and every lower-class family had its "geniuses." Some people don't realize that putting together a family history without including all of these colorful characters defeats its purpose. They are building a non-existent family of angels, instead of showing them as they really were--a family of honest, hard-working people who had the misfortune to have some family members that were "less than they should have been" (to quote a phrase of our grandparents). Personally, I'd find it terribly boring doing 200 years worth of research, and never, not once, finding a rascal on the tree.

So, you see, logic is much safer to use when dealing with ancestors. If logic is used whenever you come up against a problem, you won't find yourself saying, "My ancestor couldn't, or wouldn't, have done that, or been there, or said that." You'll know that he might have done anything at anytime during his life, things he was proud of, or sorry for--human things that we all do. But, unless you deal with him logically, and with an open mind, you will never get to know him. And that's the whole idea of looking for him in the first place, isn't it, to know him, and therefore know ourselves?

If you apply logic, then you're open to suggestions. Some may sound ridiculous at the time, but jot them down anyway and think about them. In one of my problem lines there are three of us doing this, and trading our ideas, nothing concrete as yet, but we're on the track of something--an idea triggered by a question posed by one of us. As it's shaping up now, one of my ancestors "played both sides against the middle" during the Revolutionary War, and got a land grant from one side and a pension from the other side. Brilliant maneuvering and an interesting ancestor to have hanging (I use the word loosely) from the tree.

This is the reason I said emotions had no place in research; emotions would not have found this guy for me--but logic did!

Well dear, that's the end of tonight's lecture (aren't you glad). Please don't wait so long to write. My love to the family.

Love,
Vera

COUNTY HISTORIES ARE GREAT, BUT WATCH OUT!! Their historical accounts are great but researchers must be cautious about "fairy tales" in the genealogical sections.

{V}

Augusta, Georgia

Dear Bette,

Doing some "diggin" on one of my lines the other day, I came across a book that I had checked out years ago. It gave me the idea for this letter, as you need to be told about (and warned about) this type of book: county histories.

A county's history was usually written in <u>honor</u> of something, like "it was formed 100 years ago." The local historians got together and decided to write about the events, the various wars, and the people; everyone would buy the book and they'd make money out of it, and you would have a written record of "your" county. Now, this is a great idea. After all, where would WE be without these old books to research?

But there is a catch. In order to have your family listed in the genealogical section, <u>you</u> often had to get the material together, and <u>you</u> had to pay to have it put in there. You can imagine how this turned out. Can't you just hear our New England ancestors saying, "If I've got to pay for it, I'm going to get my money's worth." And that's just what they did most of the time.

So, here you have a county history where the historical section is usually an accurate account of the early settlers and how they lived and survived all the hardships of that time, and a genealogical section that reads like a fairy tale. All the people in this section were perfect citizens--hard working, pillars of the church, non-drinkers, non-swearers, yes, perfect citizens. But that isn't realistic! We both know that every family had a black sheep (or like mine, several of them!). Great-uncle Tom who got inebriated and turned over the canoe and drowned--he's not listed. The brother who got caught smuggling--he's not there. Great-grandpa, a sea captain, who had a wife and family in BOTH ports--the second family doesn't exist in this book. And where did Aunt Marianne go?--you know, the one who already had a child when she married.

Quite frankly, when you pick up a county history you should read the first section thoroughly for clues on your family. That is where you'll read about droughts, and the blizzards, and the wars, and all the other things you need to know about the time period. That is where you get an in-depth view of their family life, their strengths, and their weaknesses--all important in building the "picture" of YOUR family.

But, the second part of the book should <u>not</u> be accepted as the absolute truth! Always check out anything found there on families that interest you. I learned this the hard way when just beginning my research. The book mentioned at the start of my letter caused me to waste three years, tracking a man who didn't exist--at least not the man who was portrayed in the book. The man I finally "found" liked a little nip now and then, and when he was "nipping" he'd do things like turning over the privy (with someone inside), and riding his horse to (and into) church, and spiking the punch at the church social (a character, to say the least!).

You can see that this is another example of not believing everything you read, but taking the time and trouble to check things out for yourself.

That's all for this time, my love to the family and write again.

Love,
Vera

{ν}

Augusta, Georgia

Dear Bette,

What is that "documentation" that I keep talking about? Well, I guess you could say that it's whatever proves the truth of your statements. That's oversimplified, of course, but there are all kinds of documents: the title for your car, your marriage license, even the deed for your land. All are proof that you have a legal right to these things. If you're asked for your birth date, nobody accepts your say so, they want to see the actual certificate issued the day you were born--that's documentation of your birth.

When you're doing research on the family, documentation is a must! Anyone can claim that an ancestor received a grant of 300 acres of land from the King of England, but a serious genealogist would have a copy of that grant included in his files. Lacking a copy machine, he would abstract the record and give his source, such as, Early Land Grants in Connecticut, (1898) Vol. 3, pg. 472, by Nathaniel Baldwin, found at the Archives in Hartford. In later years, anyone reading his material could check his sources to see if he had printed facts, or just traditions passed down through the family. That is documenting lineal ancestry.

Although the book mentioned above exists only in my head, there are many volumes on early land transactions, located in state archives, state libraries, and county courthouses. Have fun looking some up for practice and then look for your own family deeds.

Does this answer your question? Write soon, always love to hear from you.

Love,
Vera

CAN IT BE TRUE? On why not to accept a family history without sufficient proof, though many of us can identify with Bette in wanting to believe an immigrant ancestor belongs to our family tree.

{v}

Augusta, Georgia

Dear Bette,

Why are there so many errors in the Cook Family History, and how did it get published with all those mistakes in it? Well, dear, when someone decides to put together a book like this they usually don't have the money to travel around getting the needed proof. So, they make do by contacting relatives and asking them to furnish material on their various branches of the family, and include it in the book just as received. This is the cause of so many mistakes in family histories--not everyone looks for proof. All beginners seem to think the same as you did--if it's in print, it has to be true. Be thankful you've learned this lesson early in the game.

To show you the importance of accuracy--if you pick up just one wrong person, and trace his ancestry, in the four generations preceding him, you'll have traced 30 lines THAT AREN'T YOURS!

To prove a point, let me tell you about our Susannah Phinney. The Nye Book (printed 1907) had this: "Major Benjamin Nye, b. 1735, m. 1757 Susannah Phinney." As additional material was uncovered, it was included in later editions and the 1977 reprint had this: "Major Benjamin Nye, b. Sandwich, Mass. 1735, m. Barnstable, Mass. 1757 Susannah Phinney, b. Barnstable 1730-1, dau of Samuel and Hannah (Ray) Phinney." The fact that Benjamin was the only Nye in eight generations to marry a girl older than himself bothered me, but this book is well-documented, so I forgot about it.

The Phinneys were then traced, by me, back to John who married Mary Rogers, daughter of Thomas of the Mayflower. But that five-year age difference kept nagging me; it had the wrong "feel" somehow. When the Mayflower Society published its book on Thomas Rogers, it had this to say about Samuel Phinney: "We found no records of this family after the birth of the children." If they could not, where did the Nye family find them? My research began for proof that would stand up.

Two errors came to light: Barnstable vital records state that Benjamin Nye was born "in this town," and Susannah's death record said, "died 1822, age 87," which means that she was born in 1735. Sure that I was "on to something," but too far away from the source records to prove it, was frustrating. I decided that Connecticut was closer to "the scene of the crime" and passed the problem on to your brother. (Smartest thing I ever did!)

Emerson has searched the original records in various towns where Phinney families lived, and uncovered enough material to prove that this is not our Susannah (there goes the Mayflower line). In the death records of Falmouth, Massachusetts was Samuel's daughter Susannah, "d. 16 March 1812, age 81." Also the rest of Samuel's children died there. What better proof is there? But there is a bright side to this-- Emerson has also found, in Barnstable, the will of a Thomas Phinney in which he bequeathed to "my daughter Susannah Nye," and further checking on this Susannah proved that she was born 1735. The parentage of Benjamin Nye's wife is still in doubt, but IF she was the daughter of Thomas we are still descendants of Thomas Rogers through another line (Samuel and Thomas were cousins).

Remember how Grandpa Nye used to say, "If you didn't see it and you didn't hear it, then how could you say it was true?" Put this same maxim to work as you gather your material together.

End of lesson. Hi to the family and hope to hear from you soon.

Love,
Vera

{V}

Augusta, Georgia

Dear Bette,

Today we're going to talk about family tradition versus fact. When you're talking to a family member, always copy down the "traditional" part of the family history, but don't accept it as fact until you can prove it. There is usually a basis of truth in these tales, but they get embroidered every time they're repeated and end up nothing like the real thing.

A friend of mine just published her family history, all well documented, and she included a chapter on family tradition, adding the true story where she could find out what really happened. She said that was almost as much fun as researching all her lines. One of her ancestors was a ship captain from Maine. Tradition says that he left home one night to board the ship so he could leave on the early tide the next morning, that as he got into the small boat to go out to the ship he was attacked by a roving band of Penobscot Indians, fell overboard, and was drowned. Okay?

The facts were that he boarded his ship that night for the reason stated, but, during the night a hurricane hit the area, his ship broke its anchor and was smashed against the rocks; he and the entire crew were drowned--in Penobscot Bay. See how facts get twisted by continual repetition?

Every family has these traditions: that you're descended from royalty, or that your ancestor was on George Washington's staff, or was a famous scientist, or. . .or. . .or. . .. They sound good, but take them with a grain of salt unless you can prove them. And never include them in a family history as being factual unless you can back them up with proof.

No matter which phase of research you're talking about, it all goes back to the basic rule: never present as fact anything you can't prove.

Love,
Vera

YOUR GREAT-GRANDFATHER WAS A, <u>A WHAT???</u> One looks for years for a great-grandfather, finds him (finally!) in the census, and he's listed as a female! Here's what probably happened. . .

{V}

Augusta, Georgia

Dear Bette,

We've talked before about double checking information found in printed sources, but it needs to be said again--especially now that many records are being made available to researchers via the computer. The important thing to remember here is that the computer is a machine, and only prints out what has been fed into it by human hands (and THEY make mistakes!).

Several computerized census indexes have been published, and, at first glance, they are great for the family genealogist. A second glance shows you that they are sometimes full of errors! From the simple mistake of changing the surname BROWN to BRONW, they range to the more serious ones of eliminating entire counties from a state census. One page of a printed 1830 Georgia Census Index really belongs to Alabama, and about 3,400 households covering three counties is <u>left</u> <u>out</u> of an 1850 Mississippi Census Index. So, as with any other printed sources--use them, but use them cautiously!

This doesn't mean that errors are restricted to printed sources, they occur even in original records. The microfilm copy of an original South Carolina census has a young boy listed as "Yeattor." His real name? Drayton! In the same census is a male named Louisa, who was really Louis A. And Harry Evans, our Society's artist, was chasing down his great-grandfather and was <u>most</u> surprised when he found him listed in the census as "female." Why? His given name, Marion, was interchangeable between boys and girls. (Of course, it may have been because the census taker had a hard time distinguishing two-year-old boys from girls when they both wore long curls and bloomers in the 1850s!) Harry had another problem with an auntie, Wilhelmina Clifford Strozier, who showed up in the census as "Willie," male!

Many of us have sent for certified copies of records that we rely on as absolute proof in documenting our lines. Not necessarily true, "absolute." You'll find errors here, also. A few years ago I sent for the death record of Martha Wilson, d. 25 Jan 1833, widow of William Wilson, dau. of Josiah Clark and Sarah Nute. What I received was this: Martha Wilson, d. 25 Jan 1833, b. 15 Sep 1780, dau. of Josiah Wilson and Martha Clark. This is the correct Martha's date, but everything else is WRONG! The 1780 birth date is for her daughter Martha, Josiah Wilson was her son (not father), and SHE was Martha Clark before she married William Wilson. All this gotten from New England Town Records! In addition, the <u>son</u>, Josiah Wilson, never had a daughter Martha. What makes this so bad is that it is the type of documentation demanded by a lineage organization to prove your descent from a given ancestor, and since it's not worth the paper it's written on, I still can't use it.

The main thing to remember is--never, ever, accept only one source for an event! Try to locate other forms of proof, and always cross-check everything you find. In other words, play detective!

Give my love to everyone, and write again soon.

Love,
Vera

"IF ONLY I'D HAD SENSE ENOUGH TO ASK GRANDMA!" The saddest words a genealogist utters are, "if only." The treasured memories of older members of our families are golden gates to the past, if only we ask questions before it's too late!

{V}

Augusta, Georgia

Dear Bette,

This will be just a short letter as I have five million leaves waiting to be raked up. (My theory that the wind would blow them into someone else's yard didn't work!!)

All the letters going back and forth between us have dealt with finding information (how, why, when, and where) on our dead ancestors. In going through these letters, I realized that we had overlooked one very, very important source of information--our relatives who are still living! Most of the family researchers I come in contact with say to me, "I wish I'd had sense enough to question Grandma (or whoever) while she was still alive. She knew these people and could have helped me a lot." And they are right! Imagine, if you can, how much we could have found out, first hand, from all the older family members if WE had had sense enough to do it. You know that most of our relatives lived into their 80s; just think of the knowledge they had about the family in their memories of bygone years. With their passing, these memories are lost to future generations. What a waste.

What we need to do is gather up pencils, notebooks, and tape recorders, and begin visiting the older members of our family. Spend an afternoon, or several afternoons, with them, let them "walk" back through the years of memories, sharing them with you. From my own experience, all you'll have to do is ask a question occasionally, like: "Who was Alfred? The black sheep? Tell me about him, what did he do?" Or, "Was Uncle Frank really a deserter?" As they talk, a hundred questions will come to mind that you want answers to, but save some of them for another visit, as older people get tired quickly. Also, things they can't remember today they can recall another time, so take it in slow and easy stages.

Now, make a list of all your family members who are over age 60, say, and then write a list of questions that you would like to ask them about their branch of the family. When you've finished the list, it will cover several pages (I tried it!). It will really astonish you to see, written down, just how much they could help you. So, don't overlook this source of information while it's still there for you to use!

Just looked out the window and the leaves didn't blow away while we were talking, so must close and get busy. Write soon, and hugs to all.

Love,
Vera

EVERYONE WAS YOUNG ONCE! Even ancestors, though we tend to see them always as "grand-pas," not young swains.

{v}

Augusta, Georgia

Dear Bette,

Today's mail brought me a manila envelope full of papers and pictures pertaining to my Marshall family. I really got a shock at one paper written by Grandpa to his soon-to-be wife. It's really funny how youngsters get the idea that old relatives are rather stuffy and old fashioned--that they never had (or have) the same feelings about things when they were young that "we" do. What a joke on us!! My first thought was "my Grandpa <u>couldn't</u> have written this."

It was a poem from William J. Marshall to Florence Margaret Munson, dated 1890 (two years before they married). It looks like Grandpa was at sea--he worked on whaling ships and was gone for months at a time. It began, Dearest Maggie, and went on like this----

> Like brilliant diamonds set in gold
> Each eye on thine doth shine
> Thy graceful form makes me wish
> My heart was ever thine.
> Ever since I saw you first
> Fresh as the dew upon the lea
> Under thy bewitching smile
> Came burning thoughts of thee.
> Know now the love that is kindled here
> Year long year cannot deface
> Oh may you keep this memory dear
> Until I meet you face to face.
> When stormy winds are past and gone
> Shall brighter days succeed
> I try to ease a troubled mind
> Sleep is a friend indeed!
> Within these few lines
> You will in time a question find
> My question is, pray find it out
> Love is true without a doubt.

> Will

I thought it was beautiful and it gave me a new insight on my grandparents when <u>they</u> were young and courting. Grandpa was pushing 70 when I was born and my memories were of an old man, bent and crippled with arthritis, and grouchy (!). He used to tell the most glorious stories about his life at sea and all of us kids sat around with our mouths wide open. But never, never would I have dreamed that he had ever had within him the words of love written above. Doesn't pay to judge someone by his outer self, does it!!

Well dear, none of your questions got answered tonight, but wanted to share with you my feelings of pleasure at finding this "new" grandfather. Hugs to everyone.

Love,
Vera

WATCH THAT SPELLING! A name by any other spelling might belong to the same person. Let your imagination run wild--and come up with some far-out variations. Just may be the one used on that elusive record!

{V}

Augusta, Georgia

Dear Bette,

One thing for you to remember when going through records is that names were spelled just as they sounded <u>to the writer</u>. This gives you the same name spelled many different ways, so sit down and write the name every way you can think of and then look under all those spellings. An ancestor of mine spelled his own name three different ways when writing his will--Manson, Monson, and Munson. Look at your name, Kahler; it could be spelled Caler, Kaler, Kayler, or Caylor. Get the idea?

When you <u>send</u> for records this is very important; they will only check the one spelling you give them, and lots of records are missed this way. If you send three or four variations they will check all of them.

The first thing to do is to say the name out loud, and then write it the way it sounds. A few examples would be: Tomson, Tompson, Thompson, Thomson; Wait, Wayt, Weight, Waite; Wheeler, Wheler, Wealer, Whealer; Marshall, Marsill, Marshel, Martial (that one really threw me), Marshal.

Sorry this is so short, but have a busy day ahead. My love to the kids.

Love,
Vera

ON FINDING MAIDEN NAMES. Looking for maiden names of ancestors' wives can drive you up the wall, but there _are_ ways of finding them--that is, _most_ of the time, there are. The rest is luck!

{V}

Augusta, Georgia

Dear Bette,

My friend Betsey out in Los Angeles had some fabulous luck recently and I thought it would be a good subject for us to talk about. She has been searching for the maiden name and ancestry for Thankful, wife of Timothy Brown. You already have ten strikes against you by researching a surname like Brown (or Smith, or White!). All records referred to Thankful as "wife of Timothy" and never a clue as to maiden name. Finally, Betsey decided to have someone on the east coast check printed records of other families in the same area (brilliant, huh!) and they found, in the Olmstead Family History, that Thankful, daughter of Jacob Olmstead, married the Rev. Timothy Brown, and it gave their children. This list of children was exactly the same names and dates that Betsey had for her Timothy and Thankful, and all other information was the same, also. BINGO!! Betsey's search was over.

The problem of finding maiden names of wives of your male ancestors has been driving researchers up the wall for years. There are several of us who believe our female ancestors were hatched out as adults and never did have parents!! So, how do we find these wives? If they were born, died, married, or had children after your state law required these events to be recorded, it's fairly easy. Any of the above named documents should carry the maiden name of the wife in question. Our fun begins when all these events took place before records were kept, so let's see which sources might be available to us.

Never assume that the vital statistics office only has certain records. Georgia began recording deaths in 1919, but I have a certified death record from the Augusta office for a 1913 death. Always ask!!! Asking questions is one of the secrets of having success in your search.

Are there other sources? Yes! Look for her obituary in the newspaper--if she was survived by brothers or a father, _their_ surname was her _maiden_ name. If you know when her oldest child was born, then also check these same papers for a marriage record a couple of years prior to that birth. If you can find her church affiliation, then check their records for her marriage and the baptism of her children. If you don't know which church she attended, check all church records in the area, looking, of course, for the bridegroom's name (as you don't know hers). If she is buried in a city cemetery, check their records! In most cities, the city council had to approve the opening of a grave and your ancestor's family had to complete a form giving the name of the deceased, his/her age, spouse's name, where born, AND name of parents. The last item gives you her maiden name.

Don't overlook applications for military pensions. If a widow applied, she had to give all kinds of information to prove her eligibility. I have one for Sarah Marshall of Maine in which she stated, under oath, that she was born in Newbury, MA as Sarah March; their marriage intentions were recorded there; they married in Londonderry, New Hampshire in 1782 while John was on leave; after the war they settled in Norridgwock, Maine; John enlisted in the War of 1812, served in New York, and never returned home to her and their children; that he was a pensioner; and that she had been told he had died recently in New York. Then followed a list of their children.

The last one I'm going to mention is gravestones. Many times you'll find the maiden name etched on her stone--Margaret Johnson, wife of John Smith. Some just have the surname and no further data, so always check out the man buried in the grave next to her--he may have been her husband. This is another long letter I've written you! So, for now,

Love,
Vera

FEMININE NICKNAMES IN OLD RECORDS CAUSE CONFUSION. Great-great-grandfather Taylor's wife was identified as "Elizabeth" in deeds, and in marriage and death records, but in his will, g-g-gf left all to "beloved wife _Betsy_"! "Heavens!" said g-g-grandson, "Wife #2?" (No, #1, nicknamed!)

Augusta, Georgia

Dear Bette,

We won't chat too long tonight, Santa Claus is breathing down my neck and there is still so-o-o-o much to get done. This letter is about names versus nicknames, and how they confuse you when found in the records you're searching. Since we are all familiar with most men's names and how they are abbreviated, today we'll talk about the ladies.

This friend of mine, Mabel, had been searching for years trying to find the parents and birthdate for her Dicey Morgan. Mabel had Dicey's marriage to John Freeman, the obituary (which didn't help), and the cemetery records. None of the censuses for the years approximating Dicey's birth showed any Morgan with a daughter by that name. The same thing with vital records, town records, and baptisms--a dead end. Then someone answered one of her queries--and sent proof--Dicey was born Loudicia Morgan (can't say I blame her for wanting to be called "Dicey"!!!).

This type of "name problem" happens quite often in records and all of us have to be alert to any possible variations of a given name. Let's try a few. . .

We know that Sarah is also known as Sally, but had you thought she may also be Sadie? And Susannah can be Susan, but she can be Sukie, too. We know that Catherine can be Kate, but she has been found in old records as Cassie and Catty. Get the idea? I really think these nicknames were used just to confuse future researchers (and does it ever!). Some of these are familiar to all of us, but let's run through some of them, anyway. Dorothy may be Dolly; Martha possibly Patsy; Frances would be Fanny although once I found Frances called Frankie; Mary is called Polly; Margaret may be Marge, or Maggie, or Meg; Elizabeth is Beth or Lizzie; Hannah may be Ann, Annah, or Annie while the diminutive of Ann is Nancy; Lucretia is found as Lucy or Cretia; Lucinda is also shortened to Lucy sometimes; and remember our Aunt Lillian, who has always been called Lulu?

Another thing to confuse us is when a girl was given two names, say Mary Margaret, Florence Margaret, Mary Ann, or Dorothy Lillian. Some records will use the first name, some the middle name, others will use a combination of name and initial, such as Florence M. or F. Margaret. I ran into this problem with one of my ancestors; she was called Sultana on her baptism and marriage certificates, on three of her children's birth records, and on every census from 1850 to 1880. She was called Matilda on the birth records of the other four children, on her husband's death record, and she is buried as Matilda Thompson. It took years to find that she was born Sultana Matilda Wall, and that ALL the records meant the same woman.

So, when you're digging around in old records, keep your eyes AND YOUR MIND open to these variations on a given name. It might save you a lot of extra searching.

Happy holidays, and my hugs to all.

Love,
Vera

ON BARKING UP THE WRONG FAMILY TREE. Don't waste your time trying to tie yourself into a famous ancestor, just because he was famous. He may not have had any children at all!

{V}

Augusta, Georgia

Dear Bette,

I received a letter from a lady in New England last week and it gave me the subject for this letter to you. She had heard about my library on early settlers and wanted me to check on a certain man. It seems that they shared the same surname and she had decided that he was her ancestor and wanted me to help her prove it. He was very famous during the Revolutionary War and most anyone would have been proud to claim descent form him, BUT, I had to write back and tell the lady that this man had never married, had no known illegitimate children, and, therefore, she was barking up the wrong family tree!

The lesson here is that she was reversing the process of doing family research. The method that works is, you begin with yourself and work backwards. You collect documents to prove birth, marriage, and death for each generation beginning with your own, then your parents, then grandparents, and so on. Each document will give you a new clue to work with and you can proceed to the next generation. Notice that your birth record gives the names of your parents and, usually, their birthplaces--that's your new clue. Family research done any other way is often a waste of time and money.

An example of latching on to a famous name and claiming it as your own: Suppose your surname is Washington and your family came from the South. Immediately you decide that you _must_ be descended from George Washington, and you start collecting anything you can find on that surname in the area where he lived. Several years later you've spent a fortune and wasted time, only to find out that George Washington and his wife didn't have any children! Put down in black and white--doesn't that method look ridiculous? And it is! Even if such an idiotic idea had come to mind, the first thing you should have done was to research George himself, found out he had no children of his own, and then you could have started searching for your <u>own</u> Washingtons.

There is another lesson here. Don't decide at the beginning of your family research that you "must be" descended from a Mayflower passenger, a well-known early minister, a governor, or a president. Most of us descend from ordinary, hard-working people, and have not one single famous person in our lineages. Once you admit that to yourself, then genealogy becomes what it is meant to be--FUN!! No other hobby will give you as <u>much</u> fun, make you as many new friends, or give you as much satisfaction.

Well, dear, time to figure out "what's for dinner," again! Write when you have time, and hugs to everyone.

Love,
Vera

Though census takers didn't always count everyone, their lists from 1790 on are a magic timeline to trace ancestors backward through time, revealing how amazingly mobile folks were back then!

Were Your Ancestors "Counts" or "No-Counts"?

Chapter 6

HARRY EVANS '86

{V}

Augusta, Georgia

Dear Bette,

How could you say such a dumb thing--you are not a beginner anymore! You should know by now that very few of our families "always lived HERE." Most emigrated from some other state or country. Go to the library and look through any 1850 census and you'll see what I mean. As an example for you, I looked through the Gwinnett County, Georgia 1850 census and found that you could almost pinpoint a mass migration from one place to another. I found several interesting things, such as--

One man, born Virginia, wife born South Carolina, had two children born Tennessee and five children born Georgia. Another man, born North Carolina, wife born Rhode Island, had five children born Georgia, a sister-in-law born Rhode Island, and a mother-in-law born Massachusetts. Now, these families really got around!

Another was Isaac Horton, age 96, and wife, age 88. He was a Revolutionary War soldier born in Pennsylvania, wife born in North Carolina. Other Hortons living nearby and old enough to be their children, were born in North and South Carolina. (So who needed planes and trains to travel?)

These were individual families, but let's look further for a pattern of migration of several families from the same area, at about the same time. Just browsing through this census, I found three families from North Carolina and four from South Carolina who were in Georgia by 1827 and five families from North Carolina and 17 from South Carolina who were here by 1832. This set of years is important if you know that Georgia had land lotteries in those years, and free land is one of the best reasons to migrate.

Also, I found 21 families where both parents were born in South Carolina, <u>but</u>, their first child was born in Georgia in 1830. So, between ca. 1828 and 1830, we have a mass migration of families out of South Carolina into Georgia. Of course, to be able to spot these things, it helps to know the history of the area you're researching (am I repeating myself?!). In this instance, if you know Georgia history, you know that land lotteries were held in this state in 1805, 1807, 1820, 1821, 1827, and 1832. You'll also know that if "your" family was here before one of these dates, you can find published records of who drew land in each lottery.

If you still have any doubts about the feasibility of large numbers of people travelling hundreds of miles on horseback or by wagon to resettle elsewhere--forget them! In this one census, I found people from Vermont, Massachusetts, Rhode Island, Maryland, New York, Tennessee, Virginia, Pennsylvania, and even from as far away as Illinois. And, I think you'll agree that this gives new meaning to the old saying, "Where there's a will, there's a way"--and our ancestors found both!

Give everybody a big hug from me, and write when you find time.

Love,
Vera

CENSUS GIVES LOTS MORE THAN NAME, AGE, & RESIDENCE. Every ten years since 1790, Uncle Sam counted his people. Little did anyone ever realize that his lists would be used as a magic timetable to trace ancestors backward through time!

Augusta, Georgia

Dear Bette,

When we first start looking for our ancestors in census records, all we want is name, age, and residence. Few beginners realize how important it is to check the other columns on the census sheet. Each succeeding census had additional information listed--all sorts of odd things that help a family researcher.

From 1790 through 1840, only the head of the household was listed by name; others in the house-hold were broken down into age groups and sexes. There were also columns for "other free persons" and "slaves."

The 1820 census had a column which confuses the beginner: the age 16-18 group. This was added to allow officials to know how many males would be available for military service if needed. BUT, it's tricky--the same men listed in this group are also listed in the 16-26 group! So, six males in the 16-26 group, and two in the 16-18 group does not mean the man had eight sons--it means that two of the males in the 16-26 group were really between the ages of 16-18.

The 1820, 1830, and 1840 had a column for "foreigners not naturalized," allowing you to pick out newcomers to this country. The 1840 census had the added bonus of a listing of military pensioners, showing the household in which they lived. This is not of every man who had military service, only those who applied for, and received a pension from the federal government.

The 1850 census was the "biggie." It was the first time that <u>everyone</u> in a household was listed by name. It also listed age, type of work, value of real estate and personal property, and state or country of birth. For the first time you have a tentative connection between son or daughter to the parents, although defined relationships are not shown until 1880, when relationships of everyone to the head of household were listed. Thus, what you thought was a daughter may well have been a niece, cousin, or grand-daughter!!

The 1850 and onward censuses added a column showing if the couple had married within the year (the census year, naturally). The 1870 one first had columns showing if mothers or fathers were of foreign birth.

The 1880 census had several columns of interest: age prior to 1 June, month of birth if within census year, if married within the census year, and, if single, married, widowed, or divorced.

Most of the 1890 census was destroyed by fire many years ago, but a special schedule of Union veterans and widows of Union veterans of the Civil War attached to that census is still in existence, though not complete. Half of Kentucky, and most of the states from Alabama through Kansas were destroyed or misplaced. The surviving schedules are in the National Archives in Washington, DC and are available on microfilm..

The 1900 and 1910 census information is incredible: here you even learn how many children a woman had borne, and how many were still living! Can you imagine? The 1920 census was opened to the public in March 1992 and has immigration and naturalization data, birthplace of person and parents, etc.

I've just skimmed the surface on these wonderful records--bet you can't wait to get started on them, though! They're available on microfilm at libraries and in archives. We'll talk later of even more fascinating things you can find in the population schedules, and in the mortality, agriculture, and Uncle Sam's other schedules.

Love,
Vera

DOUBLE LISTING. Sometimes families moved to another county after "giving in" their family information to the census-taker, then arrived in the new home just in time to be enumerated in another census.

{V}

Augusta, Georgia

Dear Bette,

A few months ago I told you about some of the things covered in the censuses that will help a family researcher. Now it's time that you learned about the things that are guaranteed to drive you crazy (absolutely!!!). In order to evaluate the material from the census records you need to follow the same family through several censuses; that's the only way to decide how much data is accurate. Many errors exist in ages and sex, etc., etc.--another case of "it's only as accurate as the informant's knowledge." Let me give you an example of one of these "problems": double listing.

A friend of mine, Carrie Adamson, ran into this while searching for the parents of her great-great-grandmother, Sarah Louise McGarvey of Pennsylvania. All she knew was that Sarah was raised on the "McGarvey Place" near Karthaus, Clearfield County, Pennsylvania, and a check of the 1850 census there showed this family with a Sarah in the right age group...

```
Magarvey, Edward    43        census taken 29 Oct 1850
Sarah    43
Franklin  14
James     9
Caroline  11
John W.   8
Sarah     4
```

She happily "dubbed" Sarah as the daughter of Edward and Sarah...BUT...some years later (and much more experienced) she found the following listing:

```
Bellefonte, Centre County   Pennsylvania    census taken 2 Aug 1850
McGarvey, Edward    45
Sarah    44
Mary     17
William F. 14
James     11
John      8
Caroline  11
Sarah     3
```

Here's a man who lived in Centre County on 2 August, but moved to Clearfield County by 29 October when that census was taken. So, he's listed in both counties. But other clues here are the children: Mary listed in August, but gone by October; William F. had become Franklin; AND the way they are lined up under the parents. That's very important. In a census the father is first, the mother second, then the children lined up next with the oldest first, on down to the youngest. When you find them "out of line" as they are here, there IS a reason so look further.

In this case, Carrie found that Mary had married and stayed in Centre County with her new husband, also that William's middle name WAS Franklin. A family Bible found later proved that Caroline AND Sarah were not Edward's children; they were the daughters of his brother, Simon McGarvey. So, you see Edward's children were lined up in the proper way, the ones "out of line" belonged to someone else. In some cases they belonged to the husband or the wife by a prior marriage.

71

This is just one "oddity" overlooked by beginners, and will make you climb the walls trying to figure out what, or who, goes where. Will tell you others later. HAVE FUN!

Love,

Vera

SOME "WEIRD" THINGS ABOUT CENSUS RECORDS. It pays to follow a family through several censuses, copying all the data given in each, and comparing each census. There will likely be loads of errors!

Augusta, Georgia

Dear Bette,

It's a good thing that you reminded me to tell you some more "weird" things found in the census records; I had forgotten about it. As I mentioned before, it pays to follow a family through several censuses, copying down all the data given in each, then compare them and you'll find loads of errors.

For instance, a friend of mine was trying to find the parents of her grandfather. All she "knew" was his brothers and sisters, and that he was born 12 March 1863 (remember that year) in Graniteville, South Carolina. Going through the Edgefield County census for 1870, she found THE family, all names correct, all ages correct, but her grandfather was listed as age 25 and working in the mill. Can you believe it!!? On my advice she checked the 1880 and 1900 censuses, and there he was--with the right age. So wrong ages are one problem. Sometimes the person at home didn't know the right ages of the family and the census taker just estimated them--if one child was the oldest at age 16 he just put a two-year time span between all the others.

That happened for the husband and wife too, but usually for a different reason. A woman who was older than her husband wouldn't want it known, so she became one year younger than he. Or the husband of 35 had a wife of 17--he didn't want people to think he robbed the cradle, so he added a few years to her age and knocked a few off his own (that looked better, you see). If you follow through on this couple you'll find that when they've been married for 20 years this age difference doesn't matter anymore, and you now have their correct ages on a census (what fun).

Another mistake commonly made is the column listing the sex of each person. The census taker writes down: Name--Leslie--sex--male; after all, that's a boy's name. Only in this case Leslie was a girl and if you're looking for HER you've got a problem. Lots of names are interchangeable, like Vivian, Marian (with an 'o'), Charlie, etc., etc. Of course, you can't blame the census taker for all the errors, some are understandable ones, such as looking at the child with long curls, a dress, and bloomers hanging down below the dress--it just has to be a girl. But many years ago boys were dressed just like that, sometimes until they were two or three years old.

Also, the law said that the census was to be taken on the 1st of June, but we all know that everyone couldn't be listed in one day, so many were taken as late as October. Always make a record when each one was taken as it may help later to figure out ages.

Now we get to the biggie--the amount listed in the columns as "Value of Real Estate Owned," and "Value of Personal Property." Everyone knew the government was going to see these returns, and there was no way they were going to let THEM know how much of anything they owned. Then, as now, your taxes were based on what you owned.

Now you can see that research isn't all fun and games. You must have a little bit of "detective" in you, you must be able to figure out that your ancestor couldn't have had three children in 18 months since none were twins, and best of all, you must try to outwit your "crafty" ancestors when sifting through the information given by them. But there's enough fun in it that I wouldn't have missed doing it!!

Say hello to the family and write again soon.

Love,
Vera

MORTALITY SCHEDULES. If your ancestor died in the 12-month period before 1 June of 1850, 1860, 1870, or 1880, details may be in the Mortalities!

{V}

Augusta, Georgia

Dear Bette,

Thought you would catch me napping, didn't you? It just happens that I do know something about the Mortality Schedules!!

You know, of course, that censuses were taken by the federal government every 10 years from 1790 to the present; these head counts are called <u>population</u> <u>schedules</u> and that's what we consult on microfilm when we do a census search for our ancestors. We also have bonuses for some years, in <u>non-population</u> <u>schedules</u>. One of these is a mortality schedule, which was taken along with the population schedule in 1850, 1860, 1870, and 1880. It is a listing of those persons who died in the year <u>preceding</u> the beginning of the census-taking on 1 June of these years, that is, for instance, from 1 June 1849 to 1 June 1850.

In the 1850 mortality schedule, the following information is included: name, age, sex, color, whether married or widowed, place of birth, occupation, month of death, cause of death, and even the number of days ill. By 1880, the list includes length of residence in the U.S. and the place of birth of father and other! Details in all these schedules may be lengthy or short, depending on the census taker-- I've seen comments that describe circumstances of death, and even go so far as to talk about the weather, epidemics, etc.!

The 1850 mortality schedule is particularly interesting, in that it is the second time that anyone has been identified by name, before 1 June 1850, in the census schedules, <u>other</u> <u>than</u> <u>the</u> <u>head</u> <u>of</u> <u>household</u> (the first time was in the 1840 census, when living military pensioners were named). I had a neat find in the 1850 mortality schedule, to illustrate my point. The widow of one of my Revolutionary War ancestors was shown, having died in December, 1849. It gave her name, birthplace, and her age--that sent me off on a very productive search in other records. Without the mortality schedule, I may never have located her, as there were no pension papers I might have used for clues!

Another interesting thing I've found in them is that in October, 1879, my great grandparents lost three small children. All of the children were born <u>after</u> the 1870 census, and died before the 1880 one, so would not have shown on either. This find explained the gap of several years in an otherwise regular every-two-year birth pattern of their children over a 20-year period. I positively identified the family because the household visitation number is the same on the population schedule and the mortality schedule!

Where does one find mortality schedules? In 1918 and 1919 (long before there was a National Archives), the originals were distributed to non-federal repositories. The NA has succeeded in obtaining microfilms of most of them. Also, the mortality (and other nonpopulation schedules, such as agriculture, manufacturing, etc.) schedules are in many state and local libraries these days, now that microfilmed copies are offered for sale. I checked with our Augusta Public Library and found they obtained theirs from Scholarly Resources, Inc.,104 Greenhill Ave., Wilmington, Delaware 19805-1897 (1-800-772-8937)--this firm is the contractor with the National Archives and it has the schedules available from 19 states. Another firm offering certain mortality schedules on microfilm is Accelerated Indexing Systems International, 40 North Highway 89, North Salt Lake, Utah 84054 (1-800-444-0098).

Never know what you'll "dig up" next when you do genealogy!

Love,
Vera

WAS YOUR ANCESTOR A FARMER? Four agriculture schedules hold wonderful background information on mid-19th century tillers of the soil.

{V}

Augusta, Georgia

Dear Bette,

Only have time for a short note tonight, but your letter about finding an ancestor in America's "farm belt" reminded me of another schedule attached to the census (yes, dear, another one!!). Actually, there were <u>two</u> other schedules (in addition to the mortality schedule we have already discussed) attached to population schedules taken from 1850-1880--the agriculture and the industrial schedules.

The industrial schedules contain data on various businesses such as manufacturing, mining, fisheries, trading businesses, stores, and others. Those listed had an annual gross product of $500 or more; shown are the name of the company or the owner, type of business, capital invested, and the value involved in the business from labor, machinery, etc.

Your interest right now would be in the agriculture schedules. The 1850 and 1860 schedules list name of the farm owner, manager, or renter of any acreage with an annual produce worth $100 or more-- and the value of the acreage; type of machinery; produce; and livestock. The 1870 and 1880 schedules covered the same types of data except for one thing--the annual worth for each farm listed had been raised to $500 and was of three acres or more.

You can see that an ancestor who had farmland would be listed in these particular schedules, and, of course, this is another source for us to check out (all little bits of data help).

Must get busy, so will close for tonight. My love to the family.

Love,
Vera

SOUNDEX CODING SYSTEM. The rules of the soundex coding game, and how to apply them. A quick and easy way to locate those elusive ancestors who may be hard to find in censuses.

{V}

Augusta, Georgia

Dear Bette,

Well, of course I know what the Soundex Coding System is! Have used it hundreds of times and it's very simple to explain. You take the surname you want to search and use the system to come up with a code number for it. That number sends you scurrying to the Soundex Catalog to find the roll of microfilm you need to order. It works like this. . .uh, well you begin with. . .uh. . .uh. . .darn, I can't explain so you would understand! Now what do we do? I have an idea. Don't go away.

The Augusta Genealogical Society (AGS to those in the know) holds all-day workshops on a regular basis. They call them "Following Footprints is Fun." At them, classes on basic genealogical research are taught by instructors who are expert in that area. One session, on the Soundex system, is taught by Carrie Adamson. I just called Carrie to ask if I can send on her material to you, and she said, "Of course." Have fun with it!

First of all <u>Soundex</u> is a phonetic indexing system (combination of <u>sound</u> and <u>index</u>, pretty neat, huh?). It's a great way to index old records, since lots of the old-timey clerks wrote down just what they <u>heard</u>, and that was not necessarily the <u>proper</u> spelling of names and places. Soundex evens things out, because it lets you <u>hear</u> what <u>they</u> heard.

Soundex is alphabetic for the first letter of a surname, and numeric thereafter. Numbers are assigned to key letters and equivalents (with sets of like-sounding letters grouped together); vowels are not coded. But let's get to it.

<u>The Soundex Coding Guide</u>:

Code	Key Letters and Equivalents
1	b, p, f, v
2	c, s, k, g, j, q, x, z
3	d, t
4	l
5	m, n
6	r

<u>Rules of the Game and The Rules Applied</u>:

I. The first letter of a surname is <u>not</u> coded; it stands alone as the key to your Index.

<u>Example</u>: JOHNSON   J o h <u>n s o n</u>   J525

II. The letters a, e, i, o, u, y, w, and h are <u>not</u> coded.

<u>Example</u>: SWITCHERY   S w i <u>t</u> c h e <u>r</u> y   S326

III. Every surname coded for Soundex is a unit consisting of a key letter + 3 digits.

<u>Example</u>: CULVER   C u <u>l</u> v e <u>r</u>   C416

IV. Every Soundex number <u>must</u> be a 3-digit number, but not more than 3 digits.

Example: THOMPSON   T h o <u>m</u> <u>p</u> <u>s</u> o <u>n</u>   T512 (not T5125)

V. When a surname does not have sufficient codable letters, zeros are added until the coded name contains 3 digits.

Example: POTTER   P o <u>t</u> t e <u>r</u>   P360
         MOORE   M o o <u>r</u> e   M600
         LEE   L e e   L000

VI. When two identical key letters, or two or more equivalents, appear <u>side</u> <u>by</u> <u>side</u>, they are coded as one letter.

Example: McGAFFEY   M <u>c</u> G a <u>f</u> <u>f</u> e y   M210 (c,g & f,f)
         JACKSON   J a <u>c</u> <u>k</u> <u>s</u> o <u>n</u>   J250 (c,k,s)

VII. When an uncoded letter <u>separates</u> two key letters or equivalents, <u>both</u> key letters are coded.

Example: BLALOCK   B <u>l</u> a <u>l</u> o <u>c</u> k   B442 (l,l)
         KOSEZOG   K o <u>s</u> e <u>z</u> o <u>g</u>   K222 (s,z,g)

VIII. Such prefixes to surnames as "van," "Von," "Di," "de," "D'," "le," "dela," or "du" are <u>sometimes</u> disregarded in alphabetizing and in coding.

Example: D'AMICO   D A <u>m</u> i <u>c</u> o   A520
         VAN DUYN   V a n D u y <u>n</u>   D500

Now you have the surname down pat? Remember that <u>first</u> names are listed <u>alphabetically</u> within the codes, thus <u>Henry</u> Johnson would be shown before <u>Robert</u> Johnson in the J525 code section. (Note that first names are <u>not</u> soundexed.)

The system works like magic. It's a lot of fun to see how a Dutch clerk wrote names in an Ulster County (New York) militia list in the 1730s: Pitr Makrigr (M262) and Wel Soderlen (S364) are the same as Peter McGregor (M262) and Will Sutherland (S364). A German pastor in Maryland in the mid-1700s wrote in his journal that one of the Scotch-Irish brides came from the Blue Ritsch (if "Ritsch" were a surname, coded, it would be R320)--compare Ridge (R320)!

Now trot out all your surnames and code them so you're ready for the next lesson, which is how to find and use the catalogs the codes are listed in, and which years of the census are Soundexed.

Love,
Vera

M234

GOD MUST HAVE LOVED JOHNSONS, HE MADE SO MANY OF THEM! Soundex is a simple way to sort out branches of your family tree.

{V}

Augusta, Georgia

Dear Bette,

Boy, you've really been busy since receiving my letter last week about the Soundex Coding System! Fifty-two surnames coded, and correctly, too! Now you're full of questions about the catalogs-- Where do I find them? How do I use them? Are all the censuses soundexed? Which ones ARE soundexed? (Greedy, aren't you!!) You do know that genealogical research isn't meant to take the place of eating, sleeping, and all that good stuff, don't you? Or do you? Don't worry, the rest of us don't, either! But I must admit it's nice to have such an eager "pupil" (and smart, too) so let's get on with the information you wanted on the catalogs.

First of all, only four censuses are soundexed, 1880, 1900, 1910, and 1920. In 1880, only those households having children 10 years of age or younger are soundexed; in 1900, 1910, and 1920 all house-holds are soundexed. Catalogs listing microfilm rolls of censuses and soundex are available for these four federal censuses, and may be had by writing to Publications Sales Branch (NEPS), National Archives, Washington, DC 20408. It may be faster and easier for you to go to your local library and use its copies. Ask for <u>Federal Population Censuses 1790-1890</u> (for soundex info, see pages 75-85); <u>The 1900 Federal Population Census</u> (see pages 32-81); <u>The 1910 Federal Population Census</u> (see pages 19-37); and <u>The 1920 Federal Population Census</u> (see pages 16-50).

Let's begin with the 1880 Soundex. You have your surnames coded and recorded on a worksheet, right? You have your Thomas BLALOCK coded at B442 and your Henry and Robert JOHNSON at J525. And they were all in Georgia, so you turn to the Georgia listing (note that each state has a different "T" number) and see that 1880 GA is T744; B442 (BLALOCK) is on roll #7, as roll #7 covers all codes from B426 through B520. Then you check the roll number for J525 (JOHNSON) and see you have two. Roll #42 ends with J525(I) and roll #43 begins with J525(J). The (I) and the (J) indicate the first initial of the given name of the head of the household. (You remember from my last letter that surnames are coded but given names are not; given names are listed alphabetically with the code for the surname.) You would therefore check roll #42 for Henry JOHNSON (H before I) and roll #43 for Robert JOHNSON (R after J).

Now you have your Soundex Worksheet completed, and it looks like this:

Surname	Given Name	Code	"T' No.	Roll No.	Year
BLALOCK	Thomas	B442	T744	7	1880
JOHNSON	Henry	J525	T744	42	1880
JOHNSON	Robert	J525	T744	43	1880

Your next step is to order the appropriate roll through interlibrary loan, or you may wish to purchase it directly from the National Archives so you can have it permanently on hand. It will be worth waiting for, I guarantee you! Once you find the county he lived in, you can go back to your catalog and find the census roll carrying the original full entry from which the soundex card was abstracted--and reel directly to the page number dear Henry is listed on! Much more information there!!

Just in case you want to see what a Soundex card looks like, here's one from North Carolina for Henry Tysinger (T252). Bet you can't wait to see your own Henry Johnson's!

```
T252                                    North Carolina
Tysinger, Henry                            state
head of family                          vol. 7        E.D. 51
                                        sheet 4ª       line 5

W        M       40                     North Carolina
color   sex     age                        birthplace
     Davidson                           Silver Hill Twp.
       county                              M.C.D.

                     Other members of family
       Name           Relationship    Age    Birthplace
Tysinger, Sarah M          W           28      N. C.
    "       Cicero         S           18      N. C.
    "       Burges         S           15      N. C.
```

There's no need to brag about your sunny weather and make snide remarks about our rain. Rain makes things grow--all the sun does is make freckles (and I should know!). Write again and give my love to the family.

Love,

Vera

WHEN WAS YOUR ANCESTOR BORN? By consulting census records an ancestor's approximate year of birth can be computed.

{V}

Augusta, Georgia

Dear Bette,

I'm glad to see that you studied my census letters and came up with a question that I hadn't thought about. Can you figure out when a person was born by going through census records? The answer is that you can narrow it down to a certain number of years, such as 1774-1775. Begin with the 1790 census and go through the 1830 one, then "decipher" what you've found:

1790 census	under age 16	b. 1774 to 1790	(16-year time span)
1800 census	age 16 - 25	b. 1774 to 1784	(10-year time span)
1810 census	age 26 - 45	b. 1765 to 1784	(19-year time span)
1820 census	age 45 or over	b. 1775 or before	
1830 census	age 50 - 60	b. 1770 to 1780	(10-year time span)

By the 1790 census he could not have been born before 1774. By the 1830 census he could not have been born after 1780.

You now have a set of <u>possible</u> birth years for your ancestor: 1774 to 1780.

But let's see if we can narrow it down further (having fun?). You already know that his first child was born in 1799. That means he married ca. 1798. The one thing you don't know is how old he was <u>when</u> he married; the usual standard used in research is four generations to a hundred years, and that means marriage at age 25 for men. To play it on the safe side I always figure two dates, marriage at age 20 and marriage at age 25--that way you get another set of dates to work from (cautious, that me).

Here you have a man who married <u>about</u> 1798. Deduct 25 (his age) and you come up with the year 1773. Now deduct his age of 20 and have 1778. So he was born between the years 1773 and 1778, using this method. Now referring to the set of birth years derived from the census records you see two things: he couldn't have been born before 1774 (1790 census) nor was he born after 1775 (1820 census).

You now have a <u>new</u> set of possible birth years for your ancestor--1774 to 1775. AND you have narrowed the time span down to two years. Believe me, it's much easier to search a two-year supply of vital records than a 16-year one!!

So remember that if you lack proof, or records of any kind, simple logic and a lot of arithmetic will give you a <u>general</u> idea of when something might have happened (go to it; kid).

Love,
Vera

80

Chapter 7

Sources: They're Everywhere!

When you've reached the point of frustration where you think, "God only knows where I'm going to find that record," maybe Someone is trying to tell you something! Listen. Listen hard.

ON THE TRAIL OF CHURCH RECORDS. When you've reached the point of frustration where you think, "God only knows where I'm going to find that record," maybe Someone is trying to tell you something!

{V}
Augusta, Georgia

Dear Bette,

At some point in your research it becomes necessary to prove certain events that can only be found in church records. The reason for this is that in many areas church records were kept long before laws required the keeping of vital records. To locate church records, you need to find out how they were kept, where they are now, and what the records consist of for each church. Some records can be found at the church, but some were stored at a central location when space became a problem. Usually, the present minister or priest can tell you where his church's old records may be found.

While you're searching for church records, you'll come up with information that will help you understand just what kind of data the various denominations recorded. You'll learn that the Baptists seldom recorded marriages, and rarely gave the parents of the person being baptized. You'll learn that, although many of our early ancestors were very pious, they didn't consider marriage only a religious ceremony--it was also a civil contract. And you'll learn that, at one time, ministers were actually forbidden to perform the marriage ceremony! You'll learn about traveling ministers ("circuit riders") who went to settlements in the wilderness to preach sermons, baptize, preach at funerals, and marry people. They kept their records in journals, and these journals stayed with the minister wherever he went. Few of the journals survive, so the events listed in them are lost forever. One very important thing you'll learn is that these records belonged to the minister, not the church, and where he went, the records went. Many descendants of these ministers have found such records and turned them over to the church or a library, or are transcribing them for publication. Many more descendants likely just threw them away, thinking they weren't important any more.

With all the things you learned along the way, you're now wondering how anyone ever proves births or marriages from those days. Believe me, it isn't easy and sometimes it's impossible. But if you do find Minutes Books from your ancestors' church, it's worth all the trouble, for you can often fill out two or three generations worth of family charts from them.

Where do you look for old church records if they aren't at the church? Try seminary libraries (e.g., Methodist records at Drew Theological Seminary, Madison, New Jersey); special collections of colleges and universities (e.g., Methodist records at Duke University's Perkins Library); state libraries (e.g., The Connecticut State Library in Hartford has a fabulous collection of records for most of the earliest churches in the state, of any denomination); or denominational archives (e.g., the Archives of the Historical Foundation of the Presbyterian and Reformed Churches, at Montreat, North Carolina, where Gertrude Arthur found those wonderful First Presbyterian Church of Augusta records from the early 1800s that she abstracted for publication in <u>Ancestoring</u>, the AGS journal). So you see, somewhere they <u>may</u> exist, and our job is trying to find them.

By the way. the Tuolumne County (California) Genealogical Society (PO Box 3956, Sonora, CA 95370) published a great list of repositories of old church records in its July-August 1987 Newsletter. It covers the whole country, and to show you how extensive it is, it covers these denominations: Adventist, Baptist, Catholic, Congregational, Disciples of Christ, Greek Orthodox, Huguenot, Jewish, Lutheran, Mennonite, Methodist, Moravian, Schwenkfelder, Shaker, Presbyterian, Christian, and Unitarian-Universalist!

I'm sure that all of this hasn't discouraged you. By now you've learned that half of the fun of looking for our ancestors is the actual search--the tougher the better. Give my love to the family and write when you have time.

Love,
Vera

{*v*}

Augusta, Georgia

Dear Bette,

Today, we'll talk about another source for the family researcher. Although it's not usually thought of in terms of genealogy, it is a great help to those of us who live a great distance from our research area. I'm talking about the <u>National Directory of Morticians</u>. These books are updated every year and have many different items listed that are of interest to a funeral home--and invaluable to "us."

I wanted to give you a better idea of what this book consists of, so I called Elliott Sons Funeral Home, here in Augusta, and talked with Mr. David Adams. He agreed that that was the official title of the book, but said the different directories are referred to by his staff, as the Red Book, Blue Book, and Yellow Book (which, you have to agree, is easier than the title!). Mr. Adams said that his favorite is the Yellow Book, as it seems to have more information in it than the others. He told me that each state is listed alphabetically, and under each state, also in alphabetical order, is the name, address, and phone number of every funeral home in that state. There are funeral homes listed for many countries, too.

Mr. Adams also said that there are other things covered in the <u>Directory</u> that may be of interest to a researcher, such as, shipping regulations for the United States and foreign countries; a listing of the daily newspaper for many of the larger towns; lists of all veterans' cemeteries, and veterans' hospitals. At the close of our conversation he said that he would be happy to show the <u>Directory</u> to anyone who is interested (sure hope he isn't swamped with calls!). We also have a copy of the Red Book in the AGS Library, by the way.

You can see how much these books could help us to locate the death and burial of an ancestor (can't you??). Say you live in Michigan and you know that your great-grandfather died in North Carolina 50 years ago. That's it. A call to your local funeral home will give you the name and address of a North Carolina funeral home in the town where the ancestor died. Then, it's just a matter of writing a letter requesting any information they may have in their files (and don't forget to send your SASE). Isn't easier than writing "umpteen" letters trying to find out the name of any and all funeral homes in that area?

Well, that's all for today. Give my love to the family, and write soon.

Love,

Vera

DEATH NOTICES FOUND IN CONSULAR DISPATCHES. All sorts of records are kept by "Big Brother" on American citizens traveling or residing overseas. An act of 1792 ordered death records sent home--and they're all at the National Archives!

{V}

Augusta, Georgia

Dear Bette,

Haven't heard from you in several weeks, but I decided to write anyway. I had a letter from Alice last week and right away knew you had to hear what she had to say. You _did_ know that she had started family research about the same time that you did? Well, she's had a great time trying to find proof to back up family stories. And, most important, she told me about some records that I had never heard of, and may be of use to us both one day. To get on with HER story. . .

Family tradition was that there was a "lost" ancestor, and with her love of mysteries, Alice was off and running. The story was that he'd come to America from Germany in 1880 as a young man, became a naturalized citizen, and married at age 23. Soon after the birth of their first child in 1885, Johann disappeared and everyone thought he'd "run out" on his new family. They didn't want to talk about him, but Alice kept on asking questions until someone said he had owned a small home. In the town records, Alice found him listed as a dockworker and "sometime seaman." She then checked out the old records on ships leaving their port in 1885 and found that he had hired on as a seaman aboard a ship taking cargo to France.

Alice was determined to prove that no ancestor of hers would desert his family, so she and her husband decided to spend a month in Washington, DC, at the National Archives. She was sure that something would be found among the vast records there. At the end of three weeks they had found nothing, and, in desperation, they sought out one of the staff, presented the problem and asked, "Is there any other record we could try?" The man asked if they had checked the records of consular officials, and Alice is saying, "Huh?," so he explained.

Most foreign countries have an American Embassy or Consulate on their soil, and when an American dies there, an official of that country is required to make a report to the consular officials, who in turn are required to include these deaths in their dispatches sent to Washington. The report includes the name, death date and place, and, if known, where he lived in America. Therefore, if Johann had died in a foreign country, his death should be in these reports. Alice and Jim searched for three days before finding the record they'd been looking for!! Johann and several other American seamen had been killed in an accident on the docks during the unloading of cargo at LeHavre, France, and all had been buried in a small cemetery nearby. They made a trip to France, found the graves, placed a new marker on Johann's, and took pictures to show all their doubting relatives at home.

Isn't that the greatest ending? And all because Alice wasn't satisfied with family tradition (as none of us should). I was grateful that she wrote a long letter telling me about the search and about National Archives records that most of us don't know exist.

That's it for tonight as morning comes too soon for me and must get some sleep. My love to the family and write soon.

Love,
Vera

THE LDS GENEALOGICAL RECORDS COLLECTION. Over a millon and a half reels of micro-filmed genealogical data from all over the world, <u>and</u> a regularly updated index (IGI), and they're yours to use, for the asking!

{V}

Augusta, Georgia

Dear Bette,

Most of my letters have covered records that can be found in any place where public records exist. Today let's talk about another source--the records of The Church of Jesus Christ of Latter-day Saints, best known to most of us as the Mormon Church.

This Church, in 1894, founded The Family History Library at 35 North West Temple Street, Salt Lake City, UT 84150. Their object was to collect records to help persons tracing their ancestry, and they succeeded! By 1938 their collection was so large that they began putting the records on microfilm. The dream of all researchers was to be able to spend a month in Utah using these records because we knew that we'd probably never have to go anywhere else to find what we needed. Of course most of us never got there, and now we don't have to. In 1964 The Family History Library began establishing a network of Family History Centers around the country for us to use (and boy do we use them!). You can get a list of the locations and telephone numbers of those centers by writing to the address above.

There isn't any way to tell you about <u>all</u> the records they have available for you to use. Picture this (if you can!!?). At this time their holdings consist of over 225,000 volumes of books, published and un-published; over 1.6 million rolls of microfilmed records; and about 325,000 microfiche--and they continue to microfilm about 50,000 additional rolls each year (are you still there?). Can you imagine having all in one place military, land, probate, church, cemetery, birth, marriage, and death records, plus diaries, Bibles, and genealogies? Add to that list: records from Canada, England, and countries throughout Europe. And that's just the tip of the iceberg!

A more recent addition at The Family History Library, and at their Family History Centers around the country, is the installation of computers, which puts most of their records right at your finger tips. The great part about using the computers is that you (like me) don't have to know anything about them; the computer itself leads you, step by step, through the process needed to get the best results. When you decide which file you want to search it tells you which disk to put into the computer--then the main menu comes on the screen, giving you several options to choose from; choose one and then do whatever the computer says to do. For instance, you want a list of everyone with the surname "Tilestone" in Essex County, Massachusetts. You choose the disk covering the United States, put it in the computer, tell it you want Massachusetts, then Essex County, then give surname of interest. You can then tell the computer to "print out" a copy for you on the printer (neat, huh!). Once you have your copy, the computer sends you back to the main menu and you can choose other files to check. The Family History Centers around the country ask that you reserve a day and time to use their computers as so many people want to use them.

That brings me around to another recent addition to The Family History Library--the Social Security Death Index. It consists of about 40 million deaths reported to the Social Security Adminstration from 1962 through 1988. This index is heaven-sent for researchers--the data covers birth date and place, death date and place, marital status, and parents. The best news is that you can access the index (and all the others) by the use of their computers <u>and</u> get a copy from the printer.

I'd like to add that the library <u>loves</u> to receive gifts--all of your family data would be welcomed by them, though you must say that they can make copies to be circulated to their Family History Centers. But that <u>is</u> why you collected all that stuff isn't it?--to share with everyone else!!

Well, dear, suppose you write to the address above requesting a brochure listing their services and holdings, <u>and</u> the Center nearest you. Hugs to the family.

Love,
Vera

NEW ENGLAND TOWN RECORDS--THEY'RE GREAT!! A source often overlooked by researchers, these records are informative, hilarious, and sometimes shocking--but <u>never</u> boring, and "Warning Out Lists" are only some of the gems in them!

{V}

Augusta, Georgia

Dear Bette,

Your letter came this morning and I was glad to hear that the trip was so much fun, but why THERE--do you and Chuck have a "thing" about volcanoes? Just kidding, dear, one of my most prized possessions will be the pot you made with ash from Mt. St. Helena (do I get one to match?). Also glad to hear that you're ready for more research, because I have another source for you--New England Town Records.

Once you get back into the mid-1700s, you MUST get into these records. It's a source overlooked by many family researchers, as they feel that there's no need to wade through these dry, boring records of a town's history. This isn't true; they are informative, hilarious, and sometimes shocking, but <u>never</u> boring. One small town enacted a curfew law, for instance, for the "young persons of our town to govern their wild and licentious behavior," and, at the same meeting, several young people were ordered to marry. My ancestor, age 15, was ordered to marry his cousin, age 16, before their child was born (a shotgun-type wedding?). Boring? You've got to be kidding!!

Another important item you'll find in Town Records is the "Warning Out" lists. If you find an ancestor on one of these lists, please don't think he was an undesirable person; it was simply that the town couldn't afford to take charge of his family. Tax money was all they had to improve the town, the schools, the church, and assist the legal residents who might have need of help, so why waste any of it on non-residents. Remember that this was the time of the Indian Wars in New England, and many settlers of the wilderness had to flee, along with their families, to stay alive. Usually the attacks came without warning and these people had to leave everything behind. They headed for the nearest safe (?) town and arrived without the wherewithal to care for themselves--which meant they would be a burden on the taxpayers. The Town Council would meet and decide to "warn them out" of the area; they didn't care where the family went or how they survived, they just wanted them out of THEIR town. Frankly, I'd rather find my ancestor's name on the "Warned Out List" than to find that he was a member of the Town Council!!

With these lists, you can sometimes find out where the man had come from. Several years ago, a friend of mine found her ancestor on the list in a Massachusetts town; it said a ship "from Broad Bay to the Eastward" had dropped the family off. She was lost; where (or what) was Broad Bay, did I know? Luckily, I did. What is now known as Waldoborough, Maine, was originally called "Broad Bay," and a search of that area produced four generations of her family. So, you can see how important the Minutes of the Town Records can be to any family researcher. Don't forget to use them!

Well, I'd better get busy. What isn't done by noon just doesn't get done; the heat is terrible. Who would ever think of a heat wave in Augusta in September--but yesterday and today, we were (and are!) the hottest spot in the nation, the weatherman says.

Write when you have time.

Love,
Vera

IS YOUR ANCESTOR AT THE STATE ARCHIVES? Don't overlook resources at the state archives--many local records were placed there through the years for safe-keeping.

{v}

Augusta, Georgia

Dear Bette,

We're going to talk about one special place for you to go to do research on your vacation. The state archives. Most of us immediately head for the town or county where our ancestors originated--and then get disappointed when we get there. Many early records of these places were lost, lent to those who never returned them, or burned in a courthouse fire. But we don't know that until we have wasted time and effort to get there. If we had had the foresight to contact the archives in the state where we need to search, things would have been easier for us. They have lists of what records are available and for which areas in their state. My knowledge is of the Maine State Archives, but I'm sure they are not unique in the matter of collecting records from around the state and keeping them in one place (for us??).

Several years ago I wrote, asking "What material have you got in the Archives?" In reply, I received seven brochures in the mail, the first one being a history of the Archives and the services available from them, by mail or in person. Next was on records available for genealogical research, such as land records, town records, vital statistics and delayed vital statistics, and the censuses, to name a few. In this brochure I learned that there had been a Maine State Census in 1837--I now had a new source I'd never heard of before! The other five brochures went into deeper detail in describing land office records, military records, books on local history, legislative and judicial records that they may have for us to use. And all of these brochures were free!!

At the same time, my correspondent told me of two small books they had for sale at a VERY reasonable price. One was Microfilm List, Maine Town and Census Records, which consists of every type of record at the Archives from each Maine town, and the years covered. The other was Public Record Repositories in Maine, and this contains an alphabetical listing of towns and under each town the information we need is listed. When the town was incorporated, what years town and vital records were kept, where they are now (kept in Clerk's office at her home?), if indexed, if any lost or destroyed, and if the town in question has a microfilm reader for us to use--answers to questions you hardly thought to ask! Under that listing it has "Film at MSA" which tells you exactly which portion of these records is available at the Archives. There is one section for just county records, and another for what they call Deorganized Municipalities (places no longer in existence). You can bet that I ordered these two books immediately.

You can see that with the two books and the seven brochures I now know almost all the records available for Maine, and what they consist of. With this knowledge in hand before my trip is planned, I'll save a lot of time and steps when I finally manage to get my "working" vacation. So why don't you write to the archives in the state where you wish to do research this summer (address available from your local library)--they probably have the same type of literature that I received from Maine, and would be happy to send it to you. Even they prefer visitors who have planned in advance for their research trips.

Well, dear, that's it for now. Good luck on your many trips this summer--and have fun!

Love,
Vera

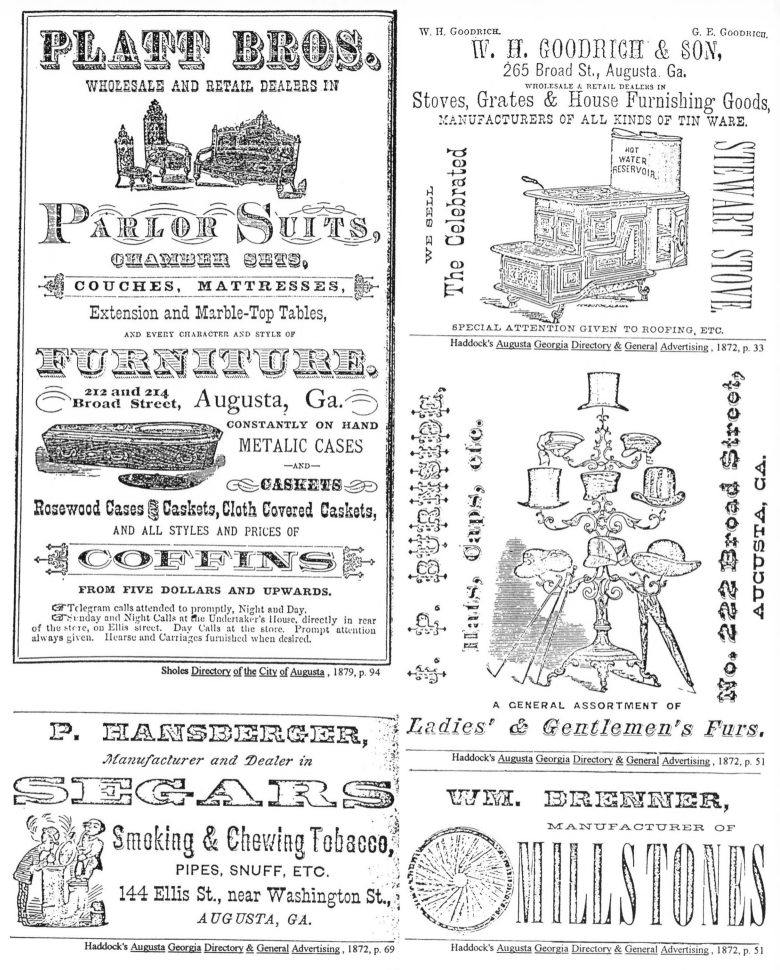

{v}

Augusta, Georgia

Dear Bette,

Have you ever thought about using city directories for towns where your research is located??? Usually we think of this source as being a help when we're searching into the 1900s, but they existed way before that. The earliest one for Augusta, Georgia was printed in 1841, and one was done in 1848 for Savannah, Georgia. So you can see that this is not a research source for genealogists to overlook. What can you expect to find in such a directory? Well. . .

Usually they are lined up in a certain order (though a lot of that depended on the time and on local custom)--in the front you'll find lists of schools, churches, hospitals, and cemeteries. In the middle there will be all kinds of businesses listed, each under a main heading such as attorneys, doctors, dry cleaners, grocers, and that type of listing. Last you'll find a complete list of residents of the area, all arranged alphabetically. In checking these surnames, be sure to look for various spellings! Beside each name you'll see other data about the person, such as "widow of John," occupation, address, and if married then in parenthesis will be the wife's name. Try checking earlier and later directories and you can get an idea of how your ancestor moved around. Also, when a person's name stops being listed, you know that one of two things has happened: he died, or he moved to another area--so that's another clue for you. And when a woman is listed as a wife one year and a widow the next, you have an approximate death date for the husband. If his place of employment, e.g. "Georgia Railroad," is shown, you can hope he retired there, and can check retirement records. Another clue is in the words after a name, "resides" and "boards." That really confused me at first, as just how many boarding houses can exist in a town? Then I realized that, in most instances, the parents "resided" at an address while one or more of their children "boarded" at the same address, so that all it meant was that grown children still lived at home.

Many city directories had very elaborate and showy advertisements in the business section. I'm sending along one from the 1876 Atlanta, Georgia directory. Isn't it great? Some of the pictures, and the wording, in these earliest ads were hilarious and it's worth going through the directory just to read them. I love to go through that section; it's more fun that what I'm supposed to be looking for!

In the early 1900s some towns added another section to their directories and this is a great help to researchers, also. It's a section of telephone numbers beginning with the lowest digits and moving up to the higher ones. Knowing how many exchanges cities have these days, it's great fun to read back when there were only four digits in a number! Beside each number is the person it belongs to and the street on which he lived, such as 100 block of Watkins Street and all the phones in that block; then the 200 block of Watkins Street and all the phones in that block, and so on, all over town. As you can see, this is a researcher's dream! The exact location of your ancestor's home sure helps if you want to look for a deed recorded at the courthouse.

Well, dear, I hope your interest has been stirred enough to start you looking at city directories in every town your search takes you to. Give the kids a hug from "ole cuz" and write when you have time.

Love,
Vera

NAME OF THE SHIP? THAT'S THE NAME OF THE GAME!! The name of your immigrant ancestor's ship and date and port of arrival are necessary before you get to the good stuff of his age, occupation, etc. on the passenger list!

{v}

Augusta, Georgia

Dear Bette,

It's funny that you should ask me about finding out which ship your ancestor arrived in this country on. It isn't that easy, as many ships only listed numbers, not names, of passengers. Also, a lot of the lists have disappeared through the years--and in many, many cases, there were none to begin with. I still haven't found out how my Munsons got here! But many of the passenger lists still in existence can be found at the National Archives in Washington, DC. Then you have many compilers, such as William Filby, Charles Boyer, Michael Tepper, Charles Banks, and others, who have published lists of early passengers. And several states have also published lists of early settlers; sometimes included is the ship they arrived on.

An easy way to find out what is in print, for a start, is to check <u>Passenger</u> <u>and</u> <u>Immigration</u> <u>Lists</u> <u>Bibliography</u> <u>1538–1900</u>, by P. William Filby. This book gives passenger lists already printed and published, and your librarian can help you obtain any of those listed that are not in your local library.

Information found on these lists will range from very little data to the man's occupation, arrival date, country of origin, age, and possibly his wife and children who came at the same time. If you know nothing except that your ancestor arrived a certain year, it's better to do the research yourself. The National Archives <u>will</u> search passengers lists if requested, but YOU must first supply them with the date of arrival, name of the ship, and the name of the port of arrival. The archives also has directories of steamships and their passengers who arrived here in America after 1890.

There are many indexes available, also, for the port of New York before 1846 and after 1897, and for Philadelphia, Boston, New Orleans, Baltimore, etc, for arrivals through the 1800s. Always keep in mind that none of these lists will give you every single passenger that arrived in this country, but they are a beginning.

There is also a move afoot to have more port arrivals soundexed--Baltimore's are already done in this way.

I hope you find your ancestor on a passenger list, as it gives you a lovely feeling to really know the name of the ship, and others who accompanied him on the journey. I haven't given up on my search yet, so don't you dare give up! Write soon.

Love,
Vera

{V}

Augusta, Georgia

Dear Bette,

As I said once before, you must study history when you're doing family research. If you don't, well, nothing you find makes sense. The question you've asked me about Loyalists could have been found in your local library, but I'll answer it, anyway.

The word Loyalist was used in America's early years to describe any settler who stayed loyal to Great Britain and the King during our Revolutionary War. These men and their families were estimated to have been at least one-third of the entire population of the original 13 colonies. They were harassed and ostracized, and their property was taken away from them. They fled to areas still under British control, such as Canada or the West Indies or went back to England, losing everything they possessed.

Many Loyalists never took up arms against their new country, and, after the war was ended, Congress recommended that the colonies restore their property to them and rescind the rigid laws concerning Loyalists. Most states refused to do either. The Loyalists then petitioned Great Britain for redress, as they lost everything because of their loyalty to the King. The Public Records Office in London, England, has records of all claims made and also the payments made to these men. They are Audit Office (A.O.) Series, American Loyalists. You have A.O. #12, which is disbursements made on the claims, and A.O. #13, which is a list of claims made. Film reel #1 of A.O. #13 is a 244-page index (and we diggers LOVE indexes!). Complete sets of this Audit Office Series are at our Library of Congress in Washington, DC, the Public Archives of Nova Scotia in Halifax, the Public Archives of Canada in Ottawa, and the LDS. Other sets may be in larger libraries around the country. It's worth checking.

I don't have enough time, or writing paper, to list everything in print on the Loyalists, but will mention two major sources. One was written to cover the Northeastern states, and the other covers the Middle Atlantic and Southern states. The first is Biographical Sketches of Loyalists of the American Revolution, 2 volumes (1864) reprinted 1979, by Lorenzo Sabine, and has 1,208 pages of information on Loyalists. The second source is a 3-volume set of books by Murtie June Clark published in 1981. This set has a total of 1,827 pages and lists the Official Rolls of Service for 35,000 Loyalists. The title is Loyalists in the Southern Campaign of the Revolutionary War. Volume 1 covers North and South Carolina, Georgia, Florida, Mississippi, and Louisiana. Volume 2 covers Maryland, Pennsylvania, Virginia, and some other colonies. Volume 3 covers the middle colonies. These two sets of books are just the tip of the iceberg! Many states published their own lists along with a short biography of the Loyalist and the property taken from him.

If you have "lost" an ancestor during this time period, there is always the possibility that he was a Loyalist. You need to go to your library and see what they have in books or old records on the Loyalists. Also, ask what is available on inter-library loan. The librarian is there to help YOU. The librarian is TRAINED to help you. Don't let that talent and training go to waste!!

Well, dear, time to start dinner (again!!), so will close for now. Hope I've stirred up your interest in this subject enough that you'll start reading everything you can find. Write when you have time.

Love,
Vera

{V}

Augusta, Georgia

Dear Bette,

One of the things you should try to find while researching your grandparents' generation and beyond, is the family Bible. Modern families have Bibles too, but not like the old ones. They were usually very large, with plenty of pages for listing all the events of a family. You may never locate one, but you have to try! They are a great source for all the dates and people you'll need as you search. Also, our ancestors used their Bibles much the same way we use a safety deposit box--everything of value was placed in it, marriage license, death certificate, even what money they had "laying around." If you find one, be sure to check between all the pages.

There are a few things to watch for, though, in order to decide how accurate the dates found in it could be. Be sure to check the date the bible was printed. One dated 1900 that has family data listed back into the 1880's needs checking; someone listed 20 years of family life all at the same time, and errors can exist, as memory is a frail thing at best.

The handwriting can give you a clue. Is it all the same? If the records cover a long time period then it's possible that the person who would have made the first entry for 1880 died in 1902--the writing after that should be in another hand. Also, look at the ink in very old Bibles. Ink was usually made at home and no two "batches" were ever the same shade. If it's all the same color, then entries were probably all done at the same time. I'm not saying that this Bible isn't an accurate account of the family, only that it needs checking if any of these things exist.

If a Bible was printed in 1859, and the owner entered his marriage in it in 1861, then listed his children's births and deaths, and maybe their marriages, and then died in 1919--his death, and subsequent listings would have to be in another's hand to give credibility to his Bible. And if they _are_ entered in another's handwriting, you usually can depend on all the data listed, from the first date to the last.

Actually, some family Bibles have found their way into libraries around the country. It gets passed on to the next generation, until it finally goes to someone who has no one to leave it to. Rather than let it get "put out with the trash" when they die, they give it to the library. So be sure to look in some of the public libraries in the area where the family lived, as well as in genealogical or historical society libraries, or in special collections in local colleges or universities.

Frankly, the chance of finding the family Bible isn't good. I've found a small mention of the Bible of one of my Marshall's (found in a cellar) and haven't located who has it yet. You just have to keep on looking and hope to get lucky one day!

Hope this provides you with another source that you probably hadn't thought of. Write when you have time, and give my love to the family.

Love,
Vera

ORIGINAL AND COPIED RECORDS. The importance of using original records, if possible. Each time a record is copied, there is a chance of error.

{**v**}

Augusta, Georgia

Dear Bette,

I've just straightened out a problem which I worked on for five years and it seemed like a good time to add to your education. This will cover the use of records: original versus copied. <u>Always</u> use original records, if possible. It saves a lot of trouble in the long run, because every time they're copied you have a chance of additional errors. I'll show you!

On my Munson line I gathered data from printed and published sources, and it all seemed to contradict whatever else I'd collected. It went this way:

Robert Munson died intestate in May 1677 (that much was accurate). Henry Putt was granted administration. The widow, as Elizabeth Putt, testified the inventory was accurate on 15 June 1677 (re-married so soon?). Robert never married. Robert was a widower. In 1684, Henry Putt was ordered to return to his wife from whom he'd been separated 11 years. Henry Putt married the widow Elizabeth Munson June 1673.

That last entry did it! You can't marry a widow four years before she becomes one. Right? The original records were the only way to clear this up, so I finally checked them. This is what I got from them:

    (1) The administration records said that <u>Eliza</u> Putt testifed about the
         inventory and that Robert was a widower.
    (2) The marriage record said that Henry Putt m. June 1673 <u>Eliza</u> Munson.

You can see what happened. Whoever copied these records for publication inserted a period after Eliza's name, making it the abbreviation for Elizabeth. And from then on his daughter Eliza became his widow Elizabeth in every book printed. This happens whenever records are copied unless you're very careful.

Never add or change <u>anything</u> in a document. "Abra" may mean Abram to you, but actually it was the abbreviated version of Abraham so you've just changed the man's first name. You must copy <u>exactly</u> everything in that original record. Don't take "11th month, 4th day, 1746/7" and write it "4 Nov 1747"--you've just changed the date of the event. Remember, in 1746/7 the 11th month was January, not November.

Original records were made at the time the event happened; <u>they</u> are your best source of infor-mation. Remember that game we played as kids where you told a story to someone and he passed it on until it reached the end of the line? If you recall, the end result was nothing like the original story. This is what happens when many records are copied and recopied--the end is never like the original record.

Goodnight for now, dear. Write soon.

Love,
Vera

RUN, DON'T WALK, TO THE ORIGINAL RECORD!! Use books and transcribed records in your research, but--where humanly possible--go to the original record for final proof. See for yourself what it really shows.

{V}

Augusta, Georgia

Dear Bette,

It's a beautiful fall morning and the last thing I want to be doing is to sit here at the typewriter talking to you (or anyone). It would be much more fun to be out raking leaves, smelling the air of autumn, listening to the birds--well, you know how much this country girl loves outdoors. But I had to tell you about a letter I had from Janice. Remember how we used to tease her brother about his name? She now tells me that it isn't an "old family name," after all. The story her parents told was that the first immigrant to this country was named Augan LeBlanc and in his honor every generation has had a son named Augan. They even had a printed genealogy on this family confirming this given name. Janice decided to trace her ancestry, even to France if possible, to get documentation wherever needed to back up the family tradition. What fun she had!!??

Every record she found in this country carried this same given name--his children's births, marriage record, deeds, his will, and cemetery records. Then she and her husband went to France, and found that the name Augan didn't appear in any LeBlanc family. They came home disappointed and then began to evaluate all the data collected here in the states, looking for clues. One thing became obvious immediately--every item they had came from a second source (books, transcriptions, etc.) Then Janice remembered some advice I had given her when she first began "digging up old bones." When you hit a brick wall in your research, ALWAYS consult the original records if humanly possible. Old handwriting is almost impossible to decode--add to that the fact that surnames were written as they sounded and not always were spelled correctly. An example is the surname of McFadden--one spelling in old records is Macpheaden (which, incidentally, Soundex codes the same as the first spelling--which often happens).

Janice and George decided to start all over and use original records only, where possible. During this second search they uncovered data proving a few minor errors in the family history, and made changes accordingly. But nothing on Augan, until they found his original will attached to a deed at the courthouse (where it would never have been expected!). They made a photocopy of it and went home to study this document--they felt that this will held the mystery of the name passed down through generations. AND THEY WERE RIGHT!! The body of the will was written in a different hand than the signature. It was a common practice in those days to have a scribe draft the body of the will, and then the testator would sign and seal the document. One of the bequests was to "my son Augan LeBlanc Junior"-- BUT--the father had, very plainly, signed his will Anjou LeBlanc, Senior. A simple transcribing error had passed a wrong given name down through several generations. It was also a careless error--if Senior was Anjou LeBlanc, then it naturally follows that Junior was named Anjou LeBlanc, too.

Janice ended her letter by saying that "honor had been restored to the family name." Her brother has gone to court and had his name and his son's name officially changed to Anjou LeBlanc.

Well, dear, it's time for me to run outside and play. Give my love to the family and write again soon.

Love,
Vera

{V}

Augusta, Georgia

Dear Bette,

You probably didn't expect to hear from me so soon after our l-o-n-g conversation last week, but just had to tell you what an idiot your "ole cuz" has been! (You might as well have the chance to tell me to practice what I preach to you!)

I've been helping a friend sort out her WARDs of Georgia. All we had was the death record of her grandfather stating that his parents were Enoch Ward and Dovie Gaddis--and we knew they all lived in northern Georgia. Of course, the first thing we did was read the 1880 Soundex since we <u>knew</u> Enoch had children under age 10 in 1880. Then we went to the 1900 Soundex--nothing in either one! Where to go next? While trying to decide that, we read the 1910 census to get the family of Enoch's son, the Rev. William Ward who did have three children by then and was living in Blue Ridge. Guess what? William was listed as "lives alone" (total frustration!) BUT, next door to him were--you guessed it--Enoch and Dovie Ward. It said that both were born in Georgia, and that both sets of parents were born in Virginia. At least we now had something...or did we? We searched the censuses for seven Georgia counties for 1850--no son Enoch for anyone (by now we're almost bald from hair-pulling). Then, a possible break came...

In Volume 7 of <u>Cherokee By Blood</u>, we found mention of a Jeremiah Ward who had sons William and Enoch and lived in Habersham County, Georgia. We were off and running again. And this is where my brain stopped working!!! I decided the easiest way to find Jeremiah was to use the Georgia census index books, 1820-1860. We found him in the 1840 index, but only "Head of Household" is named so that wasn't much help. He was in the 1860 index, so we read that census, only to find he had a son "E." (could have been Enoch, but??). He was not in the 1850 index, nor listed in the 1870 census of Habersham County, so we searched censuses for neighboring counties in North Carolina and Tennessee--nothing. All this searching and still no Enoch as a child. And why? Because I was too dumb to take my own advice!!! I've told you many times: <u>Never</u> rely on secondary sources; always use original records where possible, etc., etc. Because Jeremiah WAS in the 1850 census of Habersham County; they overlooked him when they copied names for the 1850 index. When, in final desperation, we ordered and read the 1850 census film on Habersham County, we found: Jeremiah Ward, born Virginia, wife Mariah, born Virginia, sons William and Enoch, both born Georgia, and Enoch was the right age to be the one we wanted. Then we checked the 1870 index and found them both in Lumpkin County, Georgia, read that census, and confirmed that Enoch was "ours" by the wife and child listed. And father, Jeremiah, lived next door. Of course, the searching isn't over yet. We still can't locate Enoch in Georgia in the 1880 or 1900 censuses (that guy really got around!), but we'll start with census film again soon (as soon as our eyes get "un-crossed") and have high hopes of finding him.

This wasn't an isolated case of someone being "missed" when records are copied. In the early records of Habersham County, there were four men by the surname of Ward, all there by 1817 and still there after 1820--and not one of them is in the index.

An index book, or an index in a book, is a good starting point in your research but it should never be relied on totally as I did this time. You should remember how easy it is to overlook names when you're copying thousands of them at a time. So don't forget (and I certainly won't)--use original records whenever possible!

Love,

Tia

CAN'T FIND BIRTH OR DEATH RECORDS? DON'T DESPAIR! There are many ways to come to reasonable conclusions about an ancestor's vital dates without the actual certificates in your hand! Try these on for size. . .

{v}

Augusta, Georgia

Dear Bette,

You've made a very good point--it IS hard to document a line in the absence of original vital records. Many states didn't require vital records to be recorded until the early 1900s, so that makes it even harder to prove descent from a man you believe to be your ancestor. Since you can't do it the easy way by obtaining birth or death certificates, or marriages, you must find other sources. And they do exist!

You have family papers--old letters, photographs, and Bibles--they may give you a lot of data on siblings, aunts, uncles, and grandparents. Then there are funeral home records giving age, birthplace, parents (with maiden name of mother), wife and her maiden name, death date, and burial place. From there you go to the cemetery records--a city-owned cemetery may have sexton records giving the same data as the funeral home records, and you have tombstones there, so information on them can be entered in your notes. Next, you try for an obituary in the local newspaper--this gives you his wife, children (with married surnames) and sometimes his parents, lodge and church affliations, etc., may say "he was born in Georgia and lived here for 40 years," and may tell you how old he was when he migrated. Old newspapers also carry stories of marriages and births so don't overlook that source.

Census records are a must. If possible, read the census for a period covering your ancestor from child at home to adult with his own family. This gives you his parents, brothers, sisters, and his own children--all with ages listed.

Information from all the above sources should be listed in your files, even when one source contradicts another! ALL the data given in these sources were given by informants who may, or may not, have known all the facts. Therefore, each record on its own does not constitute proof. But if several agree on date of birth or marriage, then you may be <u>almost</u> certain of the information being correct.

Next we go to a better form of proof, where data were given by an ancestor. We have deeds where both husband and wife signed (is her name the same as given above?); other deeds where he sells land "to my son John" (did he have a son John in the census?); or a deed where a man residing in Georgia sells his land in North Carolina "where I formerly lived" (does this coincide with birthplace in records above?). While we're at the courthouse looking at deeds, let's go to the Probate Office because that is where you will find more proof, and, hopefully it confirms the information you put together from the sources mentioned in the first part of this letter. Here you will find wills in which relationships are mentioned, such as "my wife Mabel," "my son John," or "my grandsons George and Jacob, sons of my deceased son George." If he had minor children, don't overlook the guardianship papers, as the court usually appointed a guardian to protect the assets of a child until he became of age. If your ancestor died intestate you need the administration papers, and these can be very informative if he left a large estate and minor children.

Here you have a will, deeds, tombstone, sexton's records, and an obituary--all stating that his wife was Mabel. BUT, was she his only wife, and mother of the children? For that you check the census records copied earlier and there is your ancestor, age 20, a son John, age 1, AND wife Mabel. Each succeeding census also calls her Mabel, so, yes, she was his only wife--and mother of their children. And, without finding an actual marriage record on file in any church or courthouse--you have "proved" that the marriage did exist.

This method takes a lot of hard work, but it's worth it all in the end if you can "build" a believ-able line of descent using these sources.

Love,
Vera

Chapter 8

Courthouses: That's Where the Good Stuff Is!

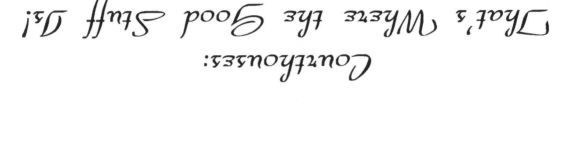

There's something in the American psyche that rebels at the "foreign territory" of a courthouse. Yet stashed there are precious records of our ancestor's deeds, wills, and other old documents we cannot do without.

ABSTRACTING WILLS IS EASY. Use a form to be sure you get everyone listed, being careful not to lose one of the children! Then go back and check again--it's important to be thorough.

{V}

Augusta, Georgia

Dear Bette,

Many years ago when this research "bug" hit me, I was at the courthouse copying some old wills --word for word--by hand (how dumb can you get??). A very nice lady showed me how to get everything needed out of the document without spending so much time doing it. I'll pass it on to you and hope it helps you as much as it did me.

What you do is write up what's called a "Will Abstract." This means that you can get all the pertinent information on a form, without having to copy all those <u>heretofores</u>, <u>whereases</u>, and <u>aforesaids</u>. Here's how:

At the top of the page you put the state, county, city, name and address of the courthouse, and the name of the court (e.g. Probate) where the record is located. Under that put the title (Will Book), volume (A), and page numbers (116-118), and if it's on microfilm, you need to put the reel number. Then you need the following things, in this order: Name of deceased, residence at the time of death, date of will, date it was probated, and name of the wife or husband. Under that list all the children (in the order they are listed in the will), then all OTHER names mentioned and the relationships to the deceased, if given. Make a list of all the bequests made (to everyone). Below that, name the executor(s) and the witnesses, then the date you copied it. NOW, go back and double-check to make sure that you've got everybody listed. You'd be surprised how many people abstracting documents do not copy witnesses and, worse yet, leave out some of the children. Would you want to be guilty of that?

You can do the same thing with deeds. Here, you would have: Who sold the land and to whom, what was paid for it, precisely where it's located, a description of the property, any relationships shown, the date the agreement was made and the date the document was filed (sometimes there are many years in between). A bonus is if you find a Renunciation of Dower Rights along with the deed; that gives you the name of the man's wife.

I finally drew up some simple forms for my own use, and am including a completed Deed Abstract and Will Abstract so you can see how they work. Both of these are from actual records, although they are not connected to our family.

Hope you're still having fun digging around in records and cemeteries. Write when you have time, and I'll try to answer your other questions soon.

Love,
Vera

WHERE WILLS MAY BE FILED. And you're missing a bet if you think they're filed <u>only</u> in the county of residence!

{V}

Augusta, Georgia

Dear Bette,

This will be just a short letter--wanted to correct a statement made to you earlier, and also share something that I've just learned (after all these years!).

In a letter to you several months ago I said, "a will is <u>always</u> found in the county where the person died, and not where he lived" (if that were somewhere else). Since then, a friend of mine has found two wills concerning her family; they were filed both where he died and WHERE HE LIVED!!! Upon asking why it was done this way, I was told that, "if you own land in the county you usually reside in, then your will must also be recorded there."

The new thing I've learned is that some states have a law that says, basically, that if you never lived in their state, but did own property there, then your will must be recorded in the county in the state where you owned the land.

So you see that a seasoned researcher can learn something new all the time. Never pays to think you "know it all," does it??!!

Well, I must finish dinner or will be in the dog house. Have fun.

Love,
Vera

GUARDIANSHIP RETURNS ARE A FAMILY RESEARCHER'S DREAM. Yearly returns to the court by an appointed guardian are full of the minutiae dear to the heart of a genealogist creating a "total ancestor" for the record.

{V}

Augusta, Georgia

Dear Bette,

It surprised me to get your last letter asking about guardianship of minor children. I'm working on that same problem right now and one thing I've learned is that not all guardianships were set up to protect orphans.

Most guardians were appointed to take care of the minor children of a man who had died leaving an estate AND a wife! That's right--he left a wife. Now you would think that the mother was capable of looking after her children and any assets their father may have left them, but the courts didn't feel that way, so they appointed a male guardian. This doesn't mean the children were taken from their mother, she still had the care of them, the guardian only took care of the estate.

As a general rule, a child under age 14 had no choices, he came under the authority of the court; but a child over age 14 could choose his guardian--subject to the approval of the court, of course. The procedure of appointing a guardian is usually the same in all states, but different courts handled the guardianships. As an example, South Carolina, Alabama, and Maine used the County Probate Court; North Carolina used the County Superior Court; some states used the County Chanercy Court. The thing to remember here is that whichever court was handling the case, it was always in the county were the child (not the guardian) lived.

The procedure was for the court to appoint a guardian, who then had to post bond with the court. After that, an inventory was taken of the estate of the deceased and a list made of all indebtedness against the estate, and all monies owed the estate. The guardian had to keep records of all monies paid into the estate and all disbursements of money until the children came of age. He also had to make annual reports to the court, and, when the children were old enough to take over, he had to give the court a final accounting of the estate, and the divisions made by him. These reports may have run over a period of several years; for instance, if a child were under age ten when his father died, you could have 11 or 12 years of annual reports. Reports that list every expenditure made on behalf of the children, such as clothing, medical, schooling, and even taxes paid on the property give you an added insight into an ancestor's life. You'd have a list of all money paid into the estate, such as a crop--raised and sold, or lease money paid on a portion of the land leased to someone else. In other words, these records are a family researcher's dream!

Well, dear, that's all I've learned so far. We'll have to share whatever we find with each other, so that we can both get smarter on this subject. Okay?? My love to all.

Love,
Vera

COUNTIES HAVE GENEALOGIES, JUST LIKE PEOPLE DO! Older counties "parented" younger ones--then the younger ones, in turn, became parents. Be sure you are seeking your ancestors in the proper courthouse.

{V}

Augusta, Georgia

Dear Bette,

In this letter we're going to discuss just how important it is to know about the state you're searching in. The main thing is to find out when the counties were formed. This may not seem like much right now, but if you get back far enough, sooner or later you'll "lose" your family. In order to find them again you must figure out where they went. But they didn't always go someplace else; sometimes the county lines changed and they were in another county--without ever having moved. Using the state of Georgia, I'll show you how this works.

From 1765-1777 Georgia consisted of 12 parishes--St. Mary, St. George, St. Thomas, St. Philip, Christ Church, St. Matthew, St. David, St. James, St. Patrick, St. John, St. Paul, and St. Andrew.

The first counties in Georgia, formed 5 Feb 1777 from these parishes, were: Burke, Camden, Chatham, Effingham, Glynn, Liberty, and Richmond. On the same date Wilkes County was formed from ceded lands of 1773.

By the end of 1796 there were 16 more counties formed, taken from a portion of these first eight counties. These were:

> Franklin County (1784) from ceded Indian lands
> Washington County (1784) from ceded Indian lands
> Greene County (1786) from Washington County
> Columbia County (1790) from Richmond County
> Elbert County (1790) from Wilkes County
> Bryan County (1793) from Chatham County
> Hancock County (1793) from Greene County and Washington County
> McIntosh County (1793) from Liberty County
> Montgomery County (1793) from Washington County
> Oglethorpe County (1793) from Wilkes County
> Screven County (1793) from Burke County and Effingham County
> Warren County (1793) from Wilkes, Burke, Columbia, Hancock, and Richmond Cos.
> Bulloch County (1796) from Bryan County and Screven County
> Jackson County (1796) from Franklin County
> Jefferson County (1796) from Burke County and Warren County
> Lincoln County (1796) from Wilkes Country

Supose you've chased your ancestor back into Warren County and can't find a single mention of him before 1793. With this list you can see that you need to check records for Columbia County, which was formed in 1790, and if unsuccessful, then to Burke, Richmond, and Wilkes Counties, all formed in 1777. Portions of these four counties were taken to form Warren County in 1793. So you might find some mention of your ancestor in the early records of four different counties--even if he hadn't moved. (Does any of this make sense to you?). Counties were formed like this in all the states, so it is important to take the time to check this information out before beginning research in that state.

I hope my explanation has made things clear to you; sometimes when I read the carbons of my letters to you I get the feeling that senility is setting in early (so ask questions while you may!). All for now, love to the family.

Love,

Vera

Chapter 9

Printed Words:
Libraries/Books/Indexes

The wonderful world of libraries and books becomes a second home to struggling genealogists, made more inviting if indexed! Properly indexed, that is, with all books factually correct and well documented. If only!

{v}

Augusta, Georgia

Dear Bette,

It was good to hear that you're going on another research trip this summer, because I have another source for you to check out. Although I'd heard of gazetteers before, it had not been my luck to have enough sense to use one. These books are wonderful for family researchers! What's a gazetteer? Well---

The formal definition is that a gazetteer is a geographical dictionary; it indexes geographical features of an area (stuffy, isn't it!). Put simply, these books list counties, townships, cities, small settlements, rivers, creeks, mountains, etc. So what's so great about that? Well, a lot of these places no longer exist on any map, or are now known by another name, therefore we have trouble locating residences of our ancestors. In early deeds, usually no town was mentioned. Instead, a deed would say "in the county of." Now counties are a large area to search, but if you can narrow down that search by using landmarks mentioned in these deeds ("south from where Bennett's Brook empties into the Little River, to the white oak 200 feet west of Murphy's ford"), you have a better chance of finding the land of your ancestor. This is where a gazetteer becomes invaluable to the researcher.

Suppose you have an ancestor that you KNOW lived in North Carolina, and you have a deed for his land that says he owned 100 acres at Cedar Mountain on Walker Creek near Little River. How do you find these landmarks in a state the size of North Carolina? Easy! You go through The North Carolina Gazetteer by William S. Powell, and you find three listings for Cedar Mountain. One is just a mountain peak in the South Mountains, the next is actually a mountain in Polk County, but the third listing is for a community named Cedar Mountain on Walker Creek, and is near Little River! You've hit pay dirt!

The most important item listed is the clue that will let you find this area on maps of today--this one goes on to say that this community was about seven miles southeast of Brevard in Transylvania County, AND Brevard can be found on any road atlas of today. Now you know where the land was located; where your ancestor settled, built his home and raised his family; and, possibly they are all buried nearby. And all this information came from a gazetteer! These books may have one other feature that helps us--they often have maps showing a lot of these old places, and one of the biggest problems a researcher has is not being able to locate maps of this earlier time period.

Now that you know about these books, be sure to use them wherever you go to search. There are large-area ones, like the Columbia Gazetteer found in most libraries (and where you can locate small communities all over the world) and we are lucky that many states have their state's gazetteer in print for us (naturally, it was done for us) and we'd be foolish to overlook this source of information. We need all the help we can get!

Hugs to the family and write again soon.

Love,

Fran

INDEXES SAVE STEPS, MONEY, AND TIME. And if they're accurate they're gifts from Heaven for the weary researcher. But be wary: Many are fraught with errors!

{V}

Augusta, Georgia

Dear Bette,

One subject that you've never asked about is <u>indexes</u>--and they ARE important when you're doing research--so let's talk about them tonight (if I can stay awake).

Without realizing it, you've probably been through several index books at the library. Patriotic organizations (such as Colonial Dames, Society of the War of 1812, Daughters of the American Revolution, United Daughters of the Confederacy, and others) publish an index periodically. On a national level, these indexes consist of the names of their members' ancestors who have been proven to have had the required service. On a state level, the indexes provide a list of the members residing in that state, along with the names of their ancestors.

At the courthouse, you find an index book for almost everything. In Clerk of Court offices (where land records are kept), there are grantor and grantee indexes--often in the same book--called a "Reversible Index."

Another type of index that is very important to researchers is one put out by genealogical and historical societies. These groups print newsletters and journals on a regular basis, and every so often publish a cumulative index covering material found in their publications over a period of years. An advertisement for this index would read something like this: <u>Index to the Journal of the Wishful Genealogical Society</u>, Vols. 1-30, 1945-1975. Sometimes, quarterly journals are indexed on a yearly basis, with that year's index appearing in, say, Vol. 5, Issue 4. Or, it may appear in the first of the next year's journal, i.e., Vol. 6, Issue 1.

Some of the best genealogical material appearing today is published in journals, so it's good to know that there are two major indexers of articles published yearly nationwide. One is <u>Periodical Source Index</u> (PERSI), and the other is <u>Genealogical Periodical Annual Index</u> (GPAI). They are indexed by author, subject, and locale, and are wonderful, wonderful helps to us. By the way, these days, with abstracting for publication often done from microfilm, at a distance from the original records, you can expect to find a Pennsylvania census, for instance, in a Florida journal! So look everywhere, in unexpected places!

You've already discovered that many of the older books you need are not available through interlibrary loan, simply because they've been out of print for years and, if lost, are irreplaceable. But did you know that many of these books have been indexed? A lot of old books didn't have an index originally, but since then, someone, somewhere, had the idea to do so, and these indexes have been printed. This is a big help for family researchers, because you now can find out IF your ancestor was listed in the book, and on which page, and then order photocopies of the pages you need through interlibrary loan, from a library holding one of the original books.

We all know that the 1790 census data is available in print and that for some states the 1800 and 1810 censuses are also. But it doesn't seem to be common knowledge that there are indexes for many states for later years; for instance, we have the Georgia 1820-1870 census indexes for our use. These give you the surname you need, and under that the head of household, of all with that surname, the page number it's found on in the reel of microfilm, the county, and sometimes the city or district. Once you locate your ancestor in one of these indexes, it's easy to find him on the microfilm. Simply go to that county and look until you find him and details of his family listed on the numbered page given in the index.

You can see by all of this that a researcher cannot function efficiently without indexes. In fact, the first thing we need to look for at a library is to see if an index has been compiled that will help save us steps (and money!). It helps save time, too. Much better to go through an index than to frustrate your way through 50 periodicals!

I hope this gives you another idea of how to "go from here to there." If it helps at all, then pass the word on to someone else. Goodnight for now.

Love,
Vera

{v}

Augusta, Georgia

Dear Bette,

You must know by now that doing family research is like putting together a large puzzle without ever having seen what the finished picture should look like. It's loads of fun, but can be frustrating too. You start with a preset idea of what and who your ancestors were and find your ideas undergoing a radical change as you progress. The first thing to do is always have an open mind--open to the fact that things could be the exact opposite of what you thought. My friend, Frances, found that out the hard way!! Let me tell you of her search for records of Patterson James (that's right! James was his surname, not his first name).

Family tradition said that Patterson was a large land owner, a well-known man in the area, and had a large family. But, she could find no records at the courthouse to back up this tradition. We decided to go back and search the index books again (some fun that was). Nothing! We laughed about finding several entries in the deed index for a James Patterson, but he didn't belong to Frances and we kept looking. We did get sidetracked on several deeds that were interesting to read. These were for lands that were being sold by the sheriff, the odd thing being that none of the 15 owners were listed in the index book (a researchers nightmare)--only the name of the sheriff. After five hours of searching we hit the jackpot!! In the index book showing the administration of estates Frances noticed her grandfather's name listed (not the name of the deceased--another stumbling block for "us") and we decided to read the entire document. Her grandfather, Patterson James, Jr., had been appointed administrator of the estate of James Patterson!! When we saw the division of the estate Frances and I just stared--how could we have been so stupid!! As heirs of James Patterson were his widow, four sons, and six grandsons--ALL WITH THE SURNAME OF JAMES! Needless to say that we went back to the index books and bought copies of every deed for James Patterson. And Frances now has documents to back up the family traditions.

There are a few lessons here. One is to always take the time to read an entire document, there are clues there that can be easily missed when you are on short time at the courthouse. We found a deed where James Patterson sold land to his daughter's new husband--if we had read the deed instead of just using the index, we would have saved a lot of time. Although the name was inverted in the body of the deed, her ancestor had signed his name as Patterson James. Another thing to remember is that many times in the index books the document is filed under the name of the sheriff (in a forced sale) and not the owner of the land confiscated or that an appointed executor or administrator, not the name of the deceased, is listed in the index.

The third thing is really the most important. Many men were given their mother's maiden name as a first (given) name to keep that family name active. Do not assume that someone wrote his name with the last (surname) first and the given name last--which is what happened in the case of the documents filed under the name of James Patterson. And when you do have an ancestor with a surname as a given name, ALWAYS keep that in mind when searching old records--and look at all records using both just to be on the safe side (may save yourself a lot of time too).

So tie a string around your finger to remember--your given name is your first name--and your surname is your last name. (Have I confused you enough?? Me too!!)

Love,
Vera

USE OF PERIODICALS IN GENEALOGY. Once a researcher has a little experience under his (or her) belt, a genealogical periodical can be of great help in finding information on the family line being traced.

{V}

Augusta, Georgia

Dear Bette,

As a researcher gets a little experience, he (or she) will find another source of information, conveyors of transcribed original records: genealogical periodicals. What's a periodical? Well, according to Noah (Webster, that is), it's something that's published on a regular basis--monthly, quarterly, semi-annually, or annually. In our field, this applies to journals and newsletters put out by historical and genealogical societies. Many people overlook them because they assume that it's all "local stuff." Not so! Material in these publications is submitted by members, and they come from all over the place.

One periodical that is familiar to me is the Maine Historical and Genealogical Recorder, published from 1884 to 1893 as a newsletter. Later, it was reprinted and placed in libraries around the country. Inside this Maine-based periodical you'll find cemetery records for Barnstable, Massachusetts; town and vital records for Ipswich, Massachusetts; early settlers of New Hampshire; early deeds and land grants; names of those buried in St. John's Burial Ground in New Brunswick, Canada; and names of early families who "went West." As you can see there was almost as much included from outside the state of Maine as there was about the state itself. Most periodicals are the same!!

And don't forget that members may place queries in these periodicals, and that has far-reaching results. I had the pleasure recently of helping a lady in Washington state who had a query in a genealogy magazine, where it was seen by a lady in Maine, and sent to me in Georgia. You can't beat that for spreading "genealogical news" around, and this happens very often.

So, the next time you go to the library, the first thing to do is grab one of these periodicals, and have yourself some fun!

Love,
Vera

USE OF ORIGINAL RECORDS VERSUS ABSTRACTS. A standing ovation to the sainted souls who abstract old records. But, remember abstracters _are_ human, and therefore not infallible!

{ν}

Augusta, Georgia

Dear Bette,

In several letters to you, I've mentioned the importance of using original source records whenever possible. When you're just starting out, that isn't always feasible, like when you live a great distance from your research point. And it wouldn't make sense to have photocopied _every_ document that bears your surname, as that would flatten your purse in a hurry! So, you rely on interlibrary loan for many things-- one of them being printed abstracts of wills and deeds. But you should use caution in using these abstracts, and I'll show you two examples, one that helped--and one that didn't!

Take my William Marshall of Lincoln County, Maine. Who were his parents? Did he own land? Was he in daddy's will? I sent for pages of deed abstracts for the time period of William's adulthood through 10 years of marriage (never saw so many Williams in one place in my life!). No help there, but in checking through later years I found where he sold land to a grandson, so I sent for a photocopy of _that_ deed. It covered two and a half acres of land, so William had acquired it somehow, right? Over a period of years, I found that his parents were Andrew and Martha, and that Martha m. 2) John Thompson, and I checked the abstract list again. I now have deeds Andrew to William, and later, Widow Thompson to William that together make up the two and half acres William sold his grandson. This is where the use of abstracts helped.

Now the example where they didn't help, but actually hindered the research. My friend, Carrie, had traced a line back to Henry Nerhut of Northumberland County, Pennsylvania. After much searching, she was positive that his father was Henry, Sr. Then she found an abstract of the will for Henry Nerhut, Sr.--and he didn't have a son, Henry!! So she started over, looking for Henry's father, but everything still pointed the same way, it had to be Henry, Sr., though the will, as abstracted, showed she was wrong. She finally assumed that Henry, Jr. _must_ be an illegitimate son of Henry, Sr. and went on to other lines. A few years ago, she was driving through the county seat where Henry, Sr.'s will was filed and she stopped to check out the original copy of the will. Guess what?? Among the list of sons _named_ _in_ _the_ _will_, there was Henry, Jr.! The abstracter had missed seeing his name. The parentage of Henry, Jr. was now solved--by consulting the _original_ document!

Honey, don't think I'm "putting down" the people who abstract old records, Heaven knows where WE would be without their work. And I shudder to think of all those hours they spend poring over huge ledgers, yellowing paper, and terrible handwriting (not _my_ idea of fun!), so that family researchers can find their ancestors. So, from my point of view, they all deserve a standing ovation! But they were and are not infallible, and they did and do overlook some things, and that's what we must remember when using their works. If you are sure that YOU are right and they are wrong, go find the original record!

Hope all the family is okay, and when are you coming South for a visit?

Love,

Vera

LIBRARIANS AND INTERLIBRARY LOAN. On the savings involved in using interlibrary loan to obtain genealogical data, rather than investing in a book. Hometown librarians are eager to help, and are prepared to "borrow" your information from another library.

{V}

Augusta, Georgia

Dear Bette,

You didn't actually BUY that book we talked about!!?? Honey, researchers can't afford to buy every book that interests them. We need money for other non-essential things--like food. You should have gotten it through interlibrary loan like the rest of us do. You never heard of interlibrary loan? You're joking. Oh, you're not joking? Well, it seems I've done it again! Why do we assume that, because WE know something, everyone else does too? Shall we talk about it?

When people first go into a public library to do research, they feel like first graders again. All those books, and all those funny numbers on the books. And just look at that huge card catalog! Where to start first? The first place to begin is with the people who work there! They know how to use the card catalog, and what those funny numbers mean (really, they do!). They'll show you how to put microfilm on the machine and they even know what to do when the film is upside down, and backwards on the reel. They know more about books and sources of material than you ever dreamed existed. They know all there is to know about their library, and they're just waiting to show you how to use it. In fact, we researchers just couldn't get along without them. THEY ARE THE GREATEST!!

Public libraries usually have a service called Interlibrary Loan. They can order for you books, census records, rolls of microfilm, and almost anything else you need for your research. To use this service you must have a card from their library, and you have to pay the postage for whatever you've ordered. Simple, isn't it? It works this way: You tell the library personnel what you need, giving title and author of the book, or the number of the census roll, or even the number of a roll on vital records of a town; then they contact their "sources" to try and find it for you. Once it's located (or not located) they call and tell you how long they can hold it for your use--this varies from 5 days to 2 weeks. Then you go to the library and go through whatever you have ordered. If you find anything pertinent to your family research you can photocopy the pages (don't forget to copy the title page, always!), and you have what you wanted--without having to pay a large sum for the entire book. Libraries usually have a machine that makes copies of microfilm, too, for your convenience, so if your family is found on census microfilm you can get a copy of that for your personal files.

You can see that, using this service, you can do loads of family research without ever leaving the town where you live, and it's easier on your pocketbook, too. One of the nicest side effects of using interlibrary loan to do research is that once you've given them all the data on what you need, you can sit back and relax; they do all the work! See--they _are_ the greatest!!!

So, head to the library with your list and try it. You'll love it.

Love,
Vera

TRASH--OR TREASURE? "Someone's trash is someone else's treasure," and no where is that more true than with books.

{V}

Augusta, Georgia

Dear Bette,

"What am I to do with all these books?" Honey, after all of our talks you shouldn't need to ask that. Just think about it. First, though, it's foolish to buy books in the hope that your family is mentioned in them. That's what interlibrary loan is all about. You borrow books through your local library's inter-library loan system, and if it has what you need, THEN you buy it. Okay?

Now, for your question. Remember that your "unwanted" books are someone else's "desperately needed" books, so an unselfish way to dispose of books it to place them out in the public eye for others to see. This means making a donation to a library in your area--see how easy it is! When you're looking around, keep one thing in mind--older libraries usually have well-stocked shelves, so try to locate a library that has been established recently and help it get going. In any area of the country there are genealogical societies, historical societies, colleges, public libraries, and lineage societies--some with their own libraries. Most of them can use donations of books, family histories, periodicals, etc. What better way to honor someone you love than to place a memorial like this in a library, with a bookplate bearing her name, as a sort of "living" memorial?

It isn't always new books that are given. The majority of books in our AGS library were given by members--some were bought new, some came off their own shelves, some were picked up at yard sales or estate sales, and some were given in memory of a loved one. Anyone can find books at yard and estate sales--just keep your eyes open. The nice thing about donating any printed matter to AGS is that the gift is tax-deductible, and the Society gives a receipt for your records. AGS enjoys a 501(c)3 tax status with the IRS, as a non-profit organization. This category has to be applied for, and approved by the IRS. AGS members have the pleasure of helping to build up their library, and an added bonus of getting a receipt to help on their tax returns. When you get ready to give away any type of literature, be sure to check around for a group with a 501(c)3 IRS tax number--that way, the donation is beneficial to both of you.

Also remember that any society in your area is in business only as long as members, and the people in the community, support the aims of the society. Any donations of books, maps, visual aids, manuscripts on your family, etc. are usually welcomed from the public. With this type of donation, dues of the members can then be used to acquire other research aids for the people of their area, or pursue other projects which will be of great benefit to their members or the community. One thing for sure--AGS and other societies that maintain private libraries simply wouldn't have much of anything on their shelves if it weren't for support through these kinds of gifts!

Guess you're glad I have to hit the kitchen now. Didn't mean to get so "windy" on this subject, but it's one close to my heart. Love and kisses to the kids, and write again.

Love,
Vera

111

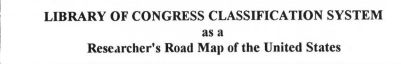

LIBRARY OF CONGRESS CLASSIFICATION SYSTEM
as a
Researcher's Road Map of the United States

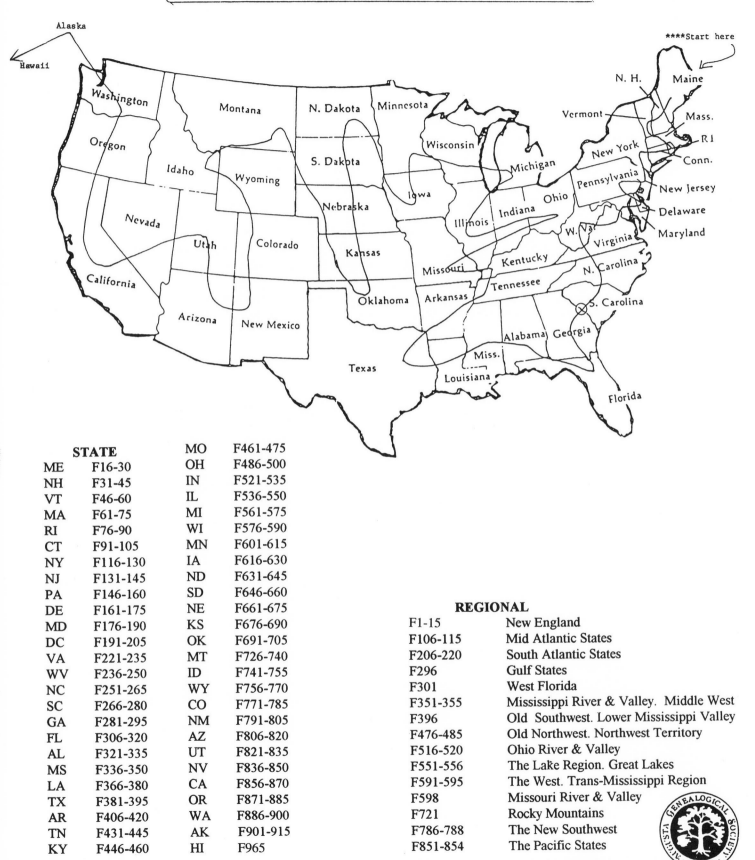

STATE			
ME	F16-30	MO	F461-475
NH	F31-45	OH	F486-500
VT	F46-60	IN	F521-535
MA	F61-75	IL	F536-550
RI	F76-90	MI	F561-575
CT	F91-105	WI	F576-590
NY	F116-130	MN	F601-615
NJ	F131-145	IA	F616-630
PA	F146-160	ND	F631-645
DE	F161-175	SD	F646-660
MD	F176-190	NE	F661-675
DC	F191-205	KS	F676-690
VA	F221-235	OK	F691-705
WV	F236-250	MT	F726-740
NC	F251-265	ID	F741-755
SC	F266-280	WY	F756-770
GA	F281-295	CO	F771-785
FL	F306-320	NM	F791-805
AL	F321-335	AZ	F806-820
MS	F336-350	UT	F821-835
LA	F366-380	NV	F836-850
TX	F381-395	CA	F856-870
AR	F406-420	OR	F871-885
TN	F431-445	WA	F886-900
KY	F446-460	AK	F901-915
		HI	F965

REGIONAL

F1-15	New England
F106-115	Mid Atlantic States
F206-220	South Atlantic States
F296	Gulf States
F301	West Florida
F351-355	Mississippi River & Valley. Middle West
F396	Old Southwest. Lower Mississippi Valley
F476-485	Old Northwest. Northwest Territory
F516-520	Ohio River & Valley
F551-556	The Lake Region. Great Lakes
F591-595	The West. Trans-Mississippi Region
F598	Missouri River & Valley
F721	Rocky Mountains
F786-788	The New Southwest
F851-854	The Pacific States

ARE YOU A "FRUSTRATED EL-SEE-ER?" Get oriented first, if you want to try the Library of Congress classification system on for size! Else, join the frustrated ranks.

{V}

Augusta, Georgia

Dear Bette,

Your last letter says loud and clear that you've joined the ranks of the "Frustrated El-see-ers!" It's a common disease among those of us library users who grew up with the Dewey Decimal system, only to be confronted these days with an increasing number of libraries going to the Library of Congress classification system. Talk about fish out of water, that's us! And when we thought all along that Heaven was sure to have a big 929 Room.

With Dewey, life was simple. 929 is Genealogy, names, insignia. Decimal breakdowns give you 929.1, Genealogy; 929.2, Family Histories; 929.3, Genealogical sources; 929.4, Personal names; 929.5, Epitaphs; 929.6, Heraldry; 929.7, Royal houses, peerage, landed gentry; 929.8, armorial bearings (coats of arms, crests, seals); and 929.9, Flags. All together on the shelves, eh?

But the Library of Congress system takes a different approach. First of all, it uses a letter at the beginning of each classification number, to designate the category to which a book belongs. F is the section we are most interested in--it's for Local History/Genealogy. Then a block of numbers is assigned to each U. S. region, and to each state, from an overall block of numbers F1-F900s. For instance, F1–15 designates New England subject matter, while F16-F30 classifies Maine books. And so on, with Alaska and Hawaii, geographically our most far-flung states, bringing up the rear.

And there's the clue. When you go back to your newly-aligned state library, think in terms of geography--"taking a walk" down the East coast, starting in Maine. From there, go across the Gulf Coast and on around the rest of the U. S., as shown on the map I'm enclosing for you. See how simple it is?

Then within each state, there's a numbering rhythm. In each state, the beginning number covers periodicals in that state; in turn, periodicals are filed alphabetically by title, within the same number. Southern Echoes is catalogued under F281 (Georgia periodicals), .S82 (alphabetically, on the second line of label). An orderly listing of subjects takes up the remainder of Georgia's numbers. All Georgia counties are under F292, alphabetically, as a further aid to us "genies."

My friend, Carrie Adamson, put the map and state designations together for use in our Society's library, as we're using the L/C system. Our members use their Researcher's Road Map of the U. S. in notebooks to take to other L/C-catalogued libraries. The Georgia Archives recently went to the L/C system, and the map has been a big timesaver in helping us find books in the new system there. Sure beats a ring-around-the-rosie, circling-the-stacks way of finding what you're looking for!

You'll find that many University Special Collections you encounter on your research trips use L/C, and more Archives are going to it all the time. Take this map with you when you travel. It's a sure cure for the Frustration Blues!

See, I told you there's help for any situation--just ask Ole Cuz. By the way, when are you coming East? Can't wait to burn the midnight oil comparing notes!

Love,
Vera

THERE _IS_ SOMETHING NEW UNDER THE SUN!! A cool way to make sure the pages of your precious books don't meet a lace-doily end!

{V}

Augusta, Georgia

Dear Bette,

It's almost midnight, but I've just got to tell you about something new on the preservation of records. If it works for large libraries, it will sure work for a home library. Down at the library last week, I was browsing through some magazines and came across the Oct-Nov 1986 issue of National Wildlife, which had an article on bugs. That's right, bugs. At first glance the story was hilarious. To get rid of bugs this way? Who'd believe that? But I photocopied it and read it again later, and it wasn't funny at all!! After you read this, maybe you can see the humor of it--for genealogy bugs to be searching for a method to kill other bugs!

The article by Noel Vietmeyer pointed out the different kinds of pests that infest books and records in homes, libraries, City Hall, and even warehouses--anywhere that paper records are stored. And these little devils don't care if they're eating a dime novel or a rare, first edition. Most of them go after the glue in old book bindings, but others like to eat leather covers (and some covers that are filled with a starch substance). Others feed on mold and mildew that grow on damp pages. Until recently, the only known way to get rid of such bugs was to spray with an insecticide--and smell the fumes for weeks afterwards. But Yale University has come up with a better idea, and I love it.

According to the story, Yale was given a set of illuminated medieval manuscripts which had been bought from an ancient monastery in southern Italy, and which had been stored for centuries in an underground vault. One professor said that they were crawling with millions of strange, wingless insects, and, "They had started from the spines and were eating into the texts and there were so many grubs that those fabulous books were turning into lace doilies." The problem was that chemical insecticides would damage the paper and might change the colors of the illuminations, so what to do now? The librarians consulted Dr. Charles Remington, head of Yale's entomology department, and he began looking for a way to debug the books. When you remember that entomology is the branch of zoology dealing with insects, you can see they made the right choice.

First, Dr. Remington identified the insects as relatives of the deathwatch beetle, and then, on a hunch, he decided to freeze several of them. He said, "After a day and a half on ice they were out cold--killed by the low temperatures." Then he and the librarians wrapped all the Italian books in plastic freezer bags and froze them for three days. Can you believe it--they were then completely free of insects!! Yale has now installed a large, walk-in freezer in the library and placed its collection of over 30,000 rare books and documents inside for "debugging." And there's a new company in Illinois that now supplies book freezers to libraries!

Dr. Remington said, "For infestations on things not living, it's the perfect pest control." Taking his remark seriously, I wrapped, in a freezer bag, that old Bible I bought at a yard sale (the one with the lace-doily pages), and froze it. It really works, and every one of my old books is going there before they're damaged further (just throw the food out!). Isn't it nice that Yale University has given those of us with libraries at home a way to protect our books and papers!!

Well, dear, must get some sleep, tomorrow comes too fast! But try freezing your old books, and let me know how it turns out. My love to all.

Love,
Vera

Chapter 10

Dictionary Time: Meaningful Meanings

Genealogists learn early not to jump to conclusions about what they find in old records, but it does jar the soul the first time you find an "inmate." Or a "crazy" ancestor. Or "d.s.p." after ggf's name!

115

SO, YOU HAVE A "CRAZY" ANCESTOR? Not to worry, it happens in the best of families! Genealogists learn early not to jump to conclusions about what they find in old records, but it does jar the soul the first time you find an "inmate."

{V}

Augusta, Georgia

Dear Bette,

You seem to be having a great time doing research, but now that you're getting into the older records you have to be careful--they are full of pitfalls for the novice. Many of the phrases and words used in colonial times had a different meaning than we give them today. One friend found her ancestor in the census and the wife was listed as a "domestic." She was outraged that this rich man had sent his wife out to work (as today's servant is a domestic), and then, researching further, found that a wife was called a "domestic." In those days it simply meant that she was "at home." And there are a lot more traps out there for the beginner (and for the more knowledgeable ones!).

My favorite is the Senior and Junior Trap. We now use these words to designate father and son, but in old records they had several uses beside the obvious ones. In a town where two men had the same name, Senior was used for the older one, and Junior for the younger one--whether they were related or not. Then in the 1600s, you'll find proof that a man named an older son "Sr." and then named a younger son "Jr." Edmund Littlefield of Maine named two sons of his Francis, Sr. and Francis, Jr., and they both married and had families (which can be confusing to the researcher!!).

Then there's "alias," which gives the impression that your ancestor had something to hide (possibly a serious crime?); it was written in old records many times. There was John Webb, alias Evered, on an early passenger list to New England. I found that "alias" meant several different things, and none criminal. It usually meant illegitimacy and the surname of the reputed father (Webb) was joined (alias) to the surname of the mother (Evered). Or, if a legitimate child was to inherit through his mother, then he often added her surname to that of his own father's. And sometimes it was used to add the surname of a stepfather to that of a deceased natural father.

Other words to watch out for are numerous. Niece could mean any female relative, but usually a granddaughter. Nephew could be an illegitimate son, but usually a grandson. A cousin could turn out to be a nephew, or an uncle. A brother could be just that, but also could be an "in-law," a lodge brother (Mason, maybe), a church brother, or even an adopted brother. And a "gentleman" wasn't necessarily well-born; the term was often used for a pensioner (one of independent income). In old wills you'll find "crazy" to describe a person; it only meant that person was ill, in poor health, but not insane. "My now wife," which protected the children of the now wife, didn't mean that the man had another wife before or after the "now wife." Then the weird occupations--tipstaff (policeman), webster (operator of a loom), hind (farm worker), boniface (innkeeper), and many more.

You'll find another tricky word in the tax lists, "inmate." This immediately makes you think that your ancestor was serving time in prison for some crime. Absolutely not!! A friend of mine had accumulated loads of material on an ancestor of hers. He was a blacksmith, a good, solid family man, an outstanding member of his church and community, and well thought of by the townspeople. Then she found him listed as an "inmate" on the 1740s tax list and wondered what had happened to this fine man-- what had made him become a criminal. With further research she found the true meaning of the word-- and had a big laugh. The word "inmate" was used then to designate a man who did not own real estate. So, quite simply, this blacksmith owned only the tools of his trade, and did not own the building where the smithy was located, therefore, he was an "inmate."

I could list many more, but your brain needs some exercise, so will let you find some for yourself. Write when you have time, and give my love to the kids.

Love,
Vera

A PIRATE--OR A PRIVATEER? The difference between a pirate and a privateer? There is a great deal of difference. Which one do you "hide" on your family tree?

{v}

                                                                    Augusta, Georgia

Dear Bette,

        I'm glad you asked the difference between a pirate and a privateer! So many family researchers find a privateer among their ancestors, and immediately "hide" him from prying eyes. They shouldn't. Privateers were men to be proud of.

        First we'll take the pirates. These men were out for personal gain only. They attacked whenever they spotted any ship riding low in the water (a sign of a full cargo, and this meant the pirates got gold, silver, gems, foodstuff, and clothes and could keep it all for their "pirate colony"). The only reason a government was behind these men was to chase them to the ends of the earth and eliminate them, making the seas safe again.

        Privateers were different in that they were commissioned by a government to do the same thing the pirates were doing, with a difference. They only preyed on enemy ships, and the captured cargo went to the government, with a percentage for the privateers--their pay, if you like.

        Article I, Section 8, of our Constitution gave Congress the right to "grant letters of marque," which authorized the seizure of ships and cargo belonging to the enemy. These letters of marque were usually granted to men who owned their own ships, as our country was too young to have built up a navy. The owners were compensated for their risks by being given a share of the "loot" taken from the enemy. This authorization lasted only until the end of a war. The United States issued many letters of marque during the Revolutionary War and the War of 1812. This custom was used by many nations around the world, but was outlawed among most nations by the Declaration of Paris in 1856; the U.S. didn't assent to the 1856 Declaration and in 1863, Congress authorized President Abraham Lincoln to permit privateering, but he did not do so. The Confederacy encouraged privateering; in 1861 President Jefferson Davis invited privateers to apply for letters of marque; I read recently (in Philip van Doren Stern's The Confederate Navy) that he issued one in May, 1861, for instance, for a private schooner from Charleston. The U.S. renounced privateering during the Spanish American War in 1898.

        If you have "men of the sea" in your ancestry it would be worth your while to check these privateer records; most are at the National Archives in Washington, DC. You'll find lists of men who were granted letters of marque, and also lists of claims made by the owners who may have lost their ships in the process of serving their country.

        You may find books at your public library concerning the privateers, if so, they make great reading. Privateers were a colorful breed of men, to say the least. Hope this answers any doubts you may have. And, tell me (confidentially) . . .do you have a privateer? Lucky you!!

                                                Love,
                                                Vera

{v}

Augusta, Georgia

Dear Bette,

    In showing a friend of mine how to set up her family on group sheets, I learned something new (see, you're never too old to learn!). I said to her that each one of the children belonging to an ancestor should have a family sheet of his own if she had data on them, and to be sure to mark q.v. by the name. She gets this blank look and says, "Why? Why not r.g. or b.l. or whatever?" That was when I realized that most of us use these abbreviations without ever knowing where they came from, or what they really mean. So, let's run through a few of them, just for fun.

    We're all familiar with A.D. (Anno Domini, Year of Our Lord), as found on deeds, wills, etc., and with ca. (circa, about), as in ca. 1820. Then we get into others, such as d.s.p. (decessit sine prole, died without issue); this one is often referred to as s.p. (sine prole, without issue). Now that's one to open your eyes if you ever see it after a name you have claimed as one of your ancestors!!

    Another is d.v.p. (decessit vita patris, died in father's lifetime). Aet. (aetatis, age, aged), is found on tombstones to show age at death. S.d. (sine die, without day) means no date is noted. V.D.M. (Verbi Dei Minister, Minister or Preacher of the Word of God) is often found in marriage records, as in "Marriage performed by the Rev. William Thompson, V.D.M."

    A very helpful abbreviation for genealogists is q.v. (quod vide, which see) which directs us to look to another part of the manuscript for further information; we often use it on family group sheets to mark a line we are following for generations.

    There were two abbreviations that drove me up the wall. One was found in a book of obituaries abstracted from newspapers; each death was listed giving the date of the newspaper. One, dated 8 October, said the man died on the 17th ult. and it was ages before I found out what that meant. Ult. (ultimo, in the preceding month) told me the man died 17 September--the month before October.

    The other one was found on a deed where a man was selling land to George Harmon Etal. My first thought was that the surname was odd, and could it be French? What a laugh I got after finding out exactly what that wording meant! It wasn't French, nor was it a surname! Et. al. (et. alia or alii, and other/s) indicated the land was being sold to George Harmon and others!

    You can see from this that we not only have FUN doing family research, we also get an education at the same time. If you've gotten back into the early years of settlement in this country it would be wise to invest in a pocket Latin dictionary...or look around at estate or yard sales for a used Black's Law Dictionary. Many of the abbreviations and phrases used in early legal documents are derived from Latin, brought to us by adoption of English Common Law in our legal system.

    Well, that's it for today (aren't you glad??); must start lunch for James. Give my love to the family and write when you have time.

Love,
Vera

ROMAN NUMERALS? EASY AS I, II, III. Roman gladiators are ancient history, Roman gods live on only in mythological tales, but genealogists still have to cope with the Roman numbering system. Not to worry, though--it's easy enough!

{v}

Augusta, Georgia

Dear Bette,

Tonight, we're going to go back and talk about a stuffy old subject--numbers. We know, of course, that numbers are important to a researcher. They tell us when an event happened, when an ancestor was born or died, even when he graduated from school.

But another _kind_ of number--the Roman numeral--is widely used by mapmakers, historians, genealogists and their societies, and many others. Don't believe me? Well, look around you. Notice that your current newsletter is Volume XII (12) and our society's latest journal was _Ancestoring_ XIII (13). The next time you're in a library, look at the Daughters of the American Revolution's _Lineage Books_; they are numbered using Roman numerals, too. In old atlases, map plates are often numbered using this system. And remember the astronomy maps we used had the hour in each section--designated by Roman numerals. Convinced? Good! Now, all we have to do is take a refresher course in order to relearn those symbols.

They taught us in school that, by combining just seven of these number symbols, we could express ALL numbers (sounds impossible, huh?). The first three symbols below are familiar to us all, but the last four are sometimes confusing (you will now learn why a hundred dollar bill is called a "C-note"). Here's the set of symbols:

I = 1   V = 5   X = 10   L = 50   C = 100   D = 500   M = 1000

Now, by combining these symbols, we can "build" as needed. Each of the examples below illustrates the way the system works: (1) When a lesser symbol _follows_ a greater one, _add_ (e.g. XI [10+1] = 11); (2) When a lesser symbol _precedes_ a greater one, _subtract_ (e.g. IX [1 from 10] = 9).

Let's practice. World War II. King George III (who was ruling in England in MDCCLXXVI-- 1776). Where did the map on the cover of _Ancestoring_ come from? That's easy--Plate CXLIII (or 143) of Volume 2, _Atlas, Official Records of the Union and Confederate Armies, 1861-1865_. An excellent article, "Sources of Irish-American Genealogy in New England," is in Volume CXXXX (140) of the July 1985 issue of _The New England Historical and Genealogical Register_. And notice the hours on an old clock! Or how about 1991 Super Bowl XXV, for a here and now use! Easy enough, isn't it.

As in the case of the NEHGR, many publications printed on a regular basis by societies-- genealogical, historical, patriotic, lineage--are numbered by this system. It's important that we researchers become very familiar with the basic seven equivalents, so we'll know how to logically look for the one "our" ancestor is in--whether it's written in Arabic _or_ Roman numeral form.

Well, dear, that's it for tonight. Talking about numbers always makes me sleepy. Hope you are all well, and hugs for everybody.

Love,
Vera

DOUBLE DATING. By now, most of us think we understand the meaning of double dating, but we may have a hard time connecting it with genealogy (except that it could have something to do with going to meetings together).

{V}   Augusta, Georgia

Dear Bette,

     Your letter came on Friday and I couldn't believe that first sentence! "Vera," you said, "I'm having trouble double dating, can you help me?" My first thought was, "At our age! Who is she kidding?" But your letter continued, "I've found g-g-g-g-g-g-g-g-great grandpa Wayte's will, but there's an error in the dates. The will was dated 5 October 1723, and probated 25 January 1723. Even a beginner like me knows that a will can't be probated until a person dies--so--what goes on here?"

     Well, dear, I'll try to explain, otherwise your charts will have wrong dates which could result in children being born before a marriage, when in reality it was a year later. And wouldn't our family just love that!

     What you have is two calendars. Prior to 1752 was the Julian (Old Style), which began on 25 March and ran through the following 24 March. Then beginning 1 January 1752 is the Gregorian (New Style), which ends 31 December. Any event occurring between 1 January and 24 March prior to 1752 should be double dated, as so: 1713/14 (this is 1713 using the Old Style calendar, and 1714 using the New Style calendar). This helps to explain the "supposed" length of time between birth and baptism; a child born 15 March 1751 and baptized 27 March 1752 was really baptized only 12 days later, not the year it seems to be at first glance.

     If you're not already confused, the next bit should do it! When the New Style calendar was adopted there were 11 extra days, so, in September of that year these days were just dropped from the calendar and 14 September 1752 became the day immediately following 2 September 1752. It also meant that everyone born between 1 January and 2 September automatically became 11 days older at that time. Isn't genealogy FUN! As a beginning researcher the following chart should be in your files:

NEW STYLE Year started 1 January 1752	MONTH	OLD STYLE Year started 25 March pre-1752
Jan	1st	March
Feb	2nd	April
March	3rd	May
April	4th	June
May	5th	July
June	6th	Aug
July	7th	Sept
Aug	8th	Oct
Sept	9th	Nov
Oct	10th	Dec
Nov	11th	Jan
Dec	12th	Feb

     Now that you've joined the rest of us digging around in musty old records you must remember one very important thing--if you can't prove "it" keep looking until you can. And never enter unproven data on your charts, unless you do so in pencil and mark it "unproven."

     Hope this has helped a little, and write again for assistance when you need it.

Love,
Vera

{v}

Augusta, Georgia

Dear Bette,

I'm glad that my letter on double dating cleared up some errors on your records--especially the one where g-g-g-g-g-g-g-g-great grandma had her twins a few months after her marriage (!!). Anyway, let's tackle your problem with John Parker.

You say that the only record you've found was "his name on a list of Ohio members of the Society of Friends (whatever that is), and a deed where he bought land, at age 43, in Ohio." Well, you now know two things, first, that he was a Quaker (a member of the Society of Friends), and second, that he lived elsewhere prior to settling in Ohio. You may not realize it, but you've hit the jackpot! Talk about beginner's luck!

Being a Quaker is the important thing here. To a family genealogist, their records are like finding the pot of gold at the end of the rainbow. But, a word of caution: copy the dates exactly as written! As a general rule, they listed dates using the number (instead of the name) of the month, with the month first. You'll find dates like this, 3-27-1733, or 3rd month, 27th day, 1733. Using the chart from my last letter, you can see that in 1733 the "3rd month" was May, so this event happened on May 27, 1733 (or as genealogists refer to it, 27 May 1733). Quaker records list births, marriages, and deaths. They also contain Letters of Transfer that say, "admitted to this Meeting from the Meeting in," and immediately, you have the town or county of prior residence. The Ohio records will show you where John Parker lived before coming to Ohio. A lot of these records have been printed in the Encyclopedia of American Quaker Genealogy, seven volumes by William Wade Hinshaw. Volumes 3 and 4 pertain to the Ohio records.

Also, if you are lucky enough to find John's marriage certificate, study it carefully. It will have the signatures of everyone who attended the wedding--friends, neighbors, and most important, relatives of the bride and groom.

One other thing. Although there were notable exceptions, generally Quakers were against war, the holding of slaves, and paying tithes to the English Church. They also refused to take oaths. Therefore, if you find any records of your Quaker ancestors fighting in a war, being owners of slaves, or holding public office, question it and do further research. This may have been another man with the same name, and not "your" ancestor.

Love,

Vera

WHAT'S YOUR LINE? ALLIED, COLLATERAL, OR DIRECT? Identifying twigs and branches in relation to the main trunk of your family tree.

{V}

Augusta, Georgia

Dear Bette,

Boy, do you come up with some great questions!! This was really a good one, though, wanting to know the difference between direct, collateral, and allied lines. At first glance they are all the same, part of your family tree, but there IS a difference. Your <u>direct</u> line is parents, grandparents, great-grandparents, and so on. Your <u>collateral</u> lines consist of those related to you by blood--uncles, cousins, nephews, and such--who are also descendants from one of your ancestors, but <u>not</u> in <u>your</u> <u>direct</u> line. Your <u>allied</u> lines are the people who married into your blood line, but are NOT your blood kin. Simple, isn't it? Okay, okay, I'll show you how it goes, using my family.

I have two sets of binders for my family, one for Marshall (paternal) and one for Nye (maternal). Each binder is set up with a family group sheet to begin each generation. Behind that, lined up in order of birth, are group sheets for each child. For instance, my parents' sheet comes first; behind that are my brother's sheets, (and all their kids,) then documentation for all. Next comes my grandparents' sheet and so on, back as far as can be proven. My Nye binders are set up the same way, the first one starting with another copy of my parents' sheet (to follow my <u>mother's</u> line). Now, in these two sets of binders (I long ago outgrew the first binder, and now have several binders in each set) I have every collateral line (along with my direct lines, of course) that can be traced, and they are all <u>blood</u> <u>kin</u>.

While collecting data on your family, you always find plenty of allied lines. These are the families that joined yours by marriage--brother's wife, uncle's wife, cousin's husband--all <u>non-blood</u> kin. So, the third set of binders covers these families and each person is followed back as far as possible, and all arranged alphabetically. There's my sister-in-law's family back to Poland, the Corbierres (my aunt's husband), the Swans (great-uncle's wife), Nutes, Spears, Harts, Benners--all married into my collateral lines "way back when."

By now you're really confused, so let me simplify it further for you. My mother is my direct line. Your mother (her sister) is a collateral connection. And that makes your father from one of my allied lines. Should I quit while I'm ahead?

Hon, all this sounds like a lot of work (and is it ever!), but when you have material on several hundred ancestors, it's the only way to keep everyone straight. Remember that your records should be kept so that you, or anyone after you, can trace an ancestor back to his origin. That is just as important as your original research, maybe more so.

I'd like to add that each sheet and document in these binders should be enclosed in a vinyl cover or envelope (like the school kids use) to protect it. These covers keep the paper clean no matter how many times it's handled, prevent tearing, keep the moisture and acid on your hands from discoloring or damaging the paper, and make it easier to turn the pages if you have stiff fingers. Also, they're perfect for those old, brittle letters that you want to save. You'll use so many of these covers that it's less expensive to buy them by the box from an office supply store, or you might try a K Mart.

Give the family my love, hug the kids, and write again when you have time.

Love,
Vera

Chapter 11

Historical Perspectives

*Putting yourself in your ancestors' shoes means
learning about events taking place at the time
they lived. History. Only now it's exciting
because you're peopling it with your own folks!*

OUR ANCESTOR FAMILIES WERE TEAMS. And from these hardy, resourceful, self-sufficient family teams were bred succeeding generations who also learned how to cope. Makes you kind of proud just to think about it, doesn't it?

{V}

Augusta, Georgia

Dear Bette,

I don't feel brainy today, so let's play a game. Let's go backward in time to when our ancestors lived and survived. Ready? You start with a list of all the modern conveniences we have to make life easy, you know, the kind we just can't do without, like gas heat, washers, dryers, shopping malls, and air conditioners. Then see how many of these our ancestors had. Right! They didn't have any of them. So, how did they live?

First they chose a piece of land, cut some of the trees for a cabin, and they planted a garden--they couldn't survive without either of these things, shelter and food. But let's go on from there. They had to be self-sufficient--no corner stores, no dairy down the road, no clothing stores around, nobody to rely on but themselves. How did they manage? Like this. . .

If they were lucky the cabin was located near a creek: if not, a spring had to be found underground and dug out for the use of the family. Once an underground spring was found, they built a stone "house" over it and used it as a cooler for perishable foods, as spring water is ice cold. Inside the cabin was a fireplace or wood stove, to provide heat and a cooking area. They planted fruit trees, berry patches, and large gardens. These gave them food--canned, dried, jammed, and jellied--for the entire year, until the next harvest. It was a lot of work, but a family seldom went hungry. Many plants were allowed to "go to seed" at harvest time, and this gave the farmer a supply of seed for the next year's garden.

Then they had farm animals, all useful in their own ways. Goats and cows gave them milk, butter, cream, and meat--they also doubled as lawn mowers. Hogs gave them pork to cure in the smoke house--and they made the greatest garbage disposals. Chickens, ducks, and geese gave them eggs and poultry to eat. They had root cellars where vegetables and fruits, such as potatoes, onions, apples, and pears were stored through the winter. From the fires the housewife saved the ashes; from the meat she saved the fat and rendered it, then she mixed the two with lye and made soap. Believe me, with lye soap around, no child was long dirty--it not only removed the dirt, but also half your skin, too!

Two or three times a year the family headed for the nearest town, to a general store to buy the things they couldn't raise for themselves. They'd buy 50-pound sacks of flour and meal, and when these sacks were empty the housewife took the seams apart and washed the sacks. When she had enough of them (all the same design) she made dresses, shirts, pillow cases, nightgowns, whatever was needed--leftover scraps were made into quilts to keep them warm during the cold months.

You can see that this family unit was self-sufficient; every member had to carry his share of the load for all of them to survive. Even the smallest child had chores to do, like feeding the chickens, or weeding the garden. Whatever a child could do to help would free someone else for another job. Each person depended on the other--a team. And from this hardy, healthy, self-sufficient family "team" was bred OUR ANCESTORS. Makes you kind of proud just to think about it, doesn't it!

Well the game is ended, hope you had fun. At least now you'll appreciate all the things you have to make life easier to live. And don't you wish (once in a while!) that we could have lived during that time period? (I AM NOT crazy!!!)

Love,
Vera

PUT YOURSELF IN THEIR SHOES. Send your mind back into your ancestor's time period if you really want to get to know him--and that means digging into history books!

{v}

Augusta, Georgia

Dear Bette,

Of course, I wasn't kidding you about history being important to genealogy! If you want to understand the people and the times, you first have to put yourself in their shoes--that means you can't interpret old records by today's standards. For instance, suppose you found this:

[Dated 1704] Robert Munson, son-in-law of Abraham Howe, asked for his release from military duty, having served one year.

From this, you decide that Robert is married to Abraham's daughter and that he must be an adult since he's obviously a married man. WRONG!!!

If you knew the terminology of that time period, the first thing you'd understand is that "son-in-law" could well mean "stepson" then; Robert was actually Abraham's stepson. That gives you the information that his real father was dead and his mother married again.

In reality, the above Robert was only 17 years old in 1704. A deposition he signed in later years proved that he was born in 1687.

Then you also have this kind of record:

Donald Franklin married Mrs. Joan Drew.

You could spend years looking for her first husband, who probably didn't even exist! That's right --in old records "Mrs." didn't <u>always</u> mean she was or had been married. The title of Mistress (Mrs.) was given to married and/or unmarried women and was a title of respect, not necessarily marital status.

Genealogy is not just going through boring old records trying to find a man who "belongs" to you. At some point you have to send your mind back into their time period to really <u>know</u> them. You have to <u>mentally</u> cook on an old wood stove, iron without an electric iron, make your clothes from feed sacks, kill (and dress) your own meat, and take your place on the bucket brigade to put out fires. Only when you can do that can you know what they did to live--and survive. What else is that but history!

This kind of history differs from what you had in school. You don't <u>have</u> to do this, so it's more interesting. Get out the books, kiddo!

Love,
Vera

WHY DID OUR ANCESTORS MOVE ABOUT SO MUCH? You'll find the answer in history books, along with lots more fascinating things about the way things were "back in the olden days." History isn't all dull dates!

{V}

Augusta, Georgia

Dear Bette,

Have you realized just how much you've learned about history in the short time you've done family research? I didn't think so. You can't do one without the other. Unless you know the history of <u>their</u> time, how can you figure out why they did the things they did? I talked about that in a recent letter to you.

Take our Francis Bristol. He married in Connecticut, his first daughter was born two years later in Wisconsin, and two years after that, another daughter--our grandmother--was born back in Connecticut. The mystery is, why did he leave home for such distant parts, and then return, in a time when travel was very hard?

I ran into the same thing while searching my Joseph Munson, who was born in Wells, Maine, move to Scarboro, Maine when very young, and later moved on to Machias, Maine. Why?? Why did this man, not married too long, who owned quite a bit of land in Scarboro, pick up and move the entire family such a distance? I finally came across a book about Scarboro in the early 1700s, and there was my answer. Over a period of years, the settlers had Indian troubles, droughts, floods, and forest fires. Their crops either burned up or flooded out--a new place was needed to settle. Several men from the area went by ship, exploring places along the coast. They finally decided on Machias and petitioned the Massachusetts government for the land. Whole families resettled in this manner, going from one state to another, founding new towns--making history.

You see why you can't do genealogy unless you also do history? When you've studied the history of an area it will become obvious why people moved on--some because of political reasons, some for religious reasons, and some for economic reasons; the reason is there in the history books. (Then some, of course, moved just because they had wanderlust!)

When a government granted land to new settlers it was no little thing--some would get up to 500 acres, the only stipulation being that they build on it and make improvements. It was a smart move on the government's side since, once a man settled in, there was now another taxpayer. And once an area was opened up, other settlers would come, too. That's how our country spread out through the years.

The word history turns some folks off. But it's not all dates and places. A lot of it is finding out simple things about the people who lived at the same time, in the same places, as your ancestors. It's fascinating to read about the way they lived back then in comparison with today, then trying to decide which you would choose if given the chance. In a nutshell, it's FUN!

Love,
Vera

OUR ANCESTORS GOT AROUND -- SO DID THEIR RECORDS!! A success story about a researcher who branched out to other states--and found her missing links.

{v}

Augusta, Georgia

Dear Bette,

Do you remember my talking about Elizabeth, the lady down in Jupiter, Florida? I met her through genealogy--she is researching Cowles and Shearer families of Augusta, Georgia. Well, she wrote the other day, on Cloud Nine because she had finally managed to trace another family. After reading her letter, it seemed to me that there is a lesson here for all of us. Never give up and never stick to just one area or one state.

We all get in a rut with our thinking sometimes--if our recent ancestors were from, say Georgia, then we search, and search, and search Georgia records (even if we hit a dead end). We forget that our ancestors traveled around almost as much as we do today. It's a good thing that Elizabeth finally realized this and began to branch out into other areas of the South, or she'd still be searching Florida records--and finding nothing!

Her search widened when she found her grandmother's death record, which said "born Harris County, Texas." Texas? Impossible! Her Raifords had never been way out there! But after running into so many blank walls in Florida, she decided to see what there was in Texas--and hit the jackpot. To show you just how many places the Raifords had been before they ended up in Florida, I'll run through her line from back as far as she knows it.

Matthew lived in Virginia and died there about 1758. His son, Phillip, moved to North Carolina and served in the Revolutionary War from that state. Phillip's son, Robert, who also served from there, moved to Augusta, Georgia, and died there in 1835. Robert's widow and their children (some were adults) left Augusta after 1841, heading west. Then the story gets good.

Robert's son, Philip Henry, born North Carolina, married in Washington, DC, moved to Harris County, Texas, returned later to Georgia, and died in Camden County, Georgia, in 1878. Philip Henry's daughter, Fannie, (grandmother to Elizabeth) was born Harris County, Texas, died West Palm Beach, Florida, and married in Beaufort, South Carolina to (get this now) Virgil Shearer, a descendant of the Cowles and Shearer lines Elizabeth had researched years ago in Georgia. Coincidence? No way. In this instance it's called research, never coincidence.

So, here we have research that covered approximately seven states in only five generations. The seventh state? That is Alabama where the Cowles and Shearer families settled after they left Augusta, Georgia, about 1817.

The lesson? To look around at states near where you found the family and to check their records. Don't have tunnel vision or you'll never have the chance to do what Elizabeth has done with her problem family.

That's it for today. Write when you have time. My love to the family.

Love,
Vera

NOTHING EVER STAYED THE SAME BACK THEN -- EVEN ADDRESSES! For instance, your ancestor bought a few acres of land in Massachusetts and come 1820, he was receiving his mail in Maine, though he had just stayed put!

{V}

Augusta, Georgia

Dear Bette,

There comes a time in researching an ancestral line when you get thoroughly disgusted--you've searched every available record in "his" state with no results beyond a certain stage. It's as if he had "hatched" as an adult, with a wife and children. What now? Well, <u>now</u> you start studying the history of the area! You have to find out things like when that state became a state, what it was before that, especially during the time your ancestor was born and growing up. This is important, because that is where you usually find the earlier records. For instance, did you know. . .

That before Maine became a state in 1820, it was called the Province of Maine in the State of Massachusetts? And, though Maine has photocopied lots of earlier records, most of them are found at the Massachusetts Archives?

That after the Revolutionary War, North Carolina granted land in the western part of THEIR STATE to many of the men who fought for independence? And that the western part they gave away is now the entire state of Tennessee?

That until after the Revolutionary War, the whole northern part of the state of Pennsylvania was claimed by Connecticut? And that records of settlers sent into this area by Connecticut are in Hartford, Connecticut?

That poor Vermont was claimed by two different states--by New Hampshire up until 1764, and then by New York in 1789 and 1790?

That records for the area east of the Penobscot River in Maine, up until the late 1700s, can be found in the provinces of New Brunswick and Nova Scotia in Canada?

You can see from this that nothing ever stayed the same back then. You bought a few acres of land in Massachusetts and, "when the dust cleared," you lived in some other state. These are the things to keep in mind when doing research: always check the history of the area to see what it used to be, then go to <u>that</u> state's records and try to find your ancestor's earlier data.

If you're confused enough for today, I'll say goodbye for now. Write soon.

Love,
Vera

COUNT YOUR BLEFFINGS. If you have in your poffeffion a copy of your gr-gr-gr-grandfather's will, consider yourself bleffed!

{V}

Augusta, Georgia

Dear Bette,

This won't be a short letter--I've spent three days transcribing some old deeds of one of my ancestors and I think my eyes are permanently crossed. If you think that today's handwriting is bad, you should try to decipher some from the 1800s. But it did give me an idea about something for my dear Bette --what to do with papers that were handwritten and illegible (besides setting fire to them!).

My method is to get a photocopy of each document, then sit down and read it, underlining with red pen any word I can't make out (don't do it on the original!). Then you go back over those words and try to decide how they fit into the rest of the sentence. Most times, the context of the sentence will give you a clue, but if you're still not sure about it, place the word in brackets. Once you've managed to make out all the underlined words, re-read the entire document several times. If it still doesn't make sense, you have a mistake. Try again. Very seldom do you manage to decipher every word, but those you do get give you a good overall idea of what the document says.

Another problem is the old script where the lower case letters u, n, m, w, and v all look alike. If you're not sure about which is correct try the word using each letter--sometimes you get lucky. Then their capital letters back then--they are a researcher's nightmare! The capital letters T, J, I, L, F, and S may all look similar. Here you have to look for the cross stroke which makes the F, and remember that the capital letter J didn't usually extend below the line of writing. Again, if in doubt try each one to see which capital letter makes a logical word.

The most fun you'll have is with the long s, written so it resembles a lower case f. It causes no end of confusion to a novice. Suppose you have a sentence that begins this way: "He and his heirs will keep poffeffion of the land until..." Now there just isn't any word in the English language like "poffeffion." If you know about the long s, you know the correct word is "possession," but if you've never heard of this practice, then you must (again) approach the sentence with logic--if that word is wrong just what is the right word to fit in that particular sentence, remembering that the sentence must make sense! Another problem is that, in a double s, the second s may be written as an s, thus Jesse becomes Jefse. Haven't you seen lots of Jefses in published abstracts?

Actually, a lot of this is logical conclusion; most old documents conformed to a set of rules. After telling who he was and where he lived, a deedmaker would go on to describe the land transaction in detail --size of acreage, who owned the land on each side, and sometimes where the seller got it in the first place. Same way with wills. After all the usual "of sound mind" and such, the willmaker began making his bequests, "Item 1" and so on. If you're aware of this conformity, you will have less trouble figuring out the rest, because you KNOW what the first part says and you now have a sample of handwriting to compare with the rest of the document--you can see how a man makes his capital I or S in the beginning.

You can see from this that patience is needed to get an accurate interpretation--also a good magnifying glass! But the end result is worth all the trouble, as you now have something that anyone can read. Have fun with yours!

Love,
Vera

{v}

Augusta, Georgia

Dear Bette,

Leave it to you to come up with something I hadn't used in years! Thank goodness my files hold a bit on almost every subject. The answer to your question, "What are ear marks?" was there, just had to dig a little for it.

In the early days of this country there weren't many fences, and you had to have some way to identify your stock from that belonging to others. The only animal actually branded, as they do today, was the horse, and you had to record with the officials a complete description: color, mare or stallion, and the brand. One I found said, " grey mare with black mane, white star on forehead, and branded with ye letters N.P. on ye hind part of buttock under ye tayle" (bet the horse loved that!).

To get back to your question. Back then animals were allowed, by law, to run loose "after being properly marked as ye law directs." Your name and mark were entered in the town's record book and couldn't be used by anyone else. That resulted in many variations of the same "ear mark." A few found in Kittery, Maine records and quoted as written were: "a swallow tayle cut in ye right ear"; "a swallow tayle cut in ye right ear and a hole in ye same"; "a swallow tayle cut in ye right ear and a half penny cut in ye under side of ye left ear." See how they each began with the swallow tayle and then added something different to make this mark distinctively theirs?

Yes, dear, I know, the poor little cow (or goat, or piggy, or whatever)! Don't lose any sleep over it; it happened three hundred years ago. Hope to have a letter from you soon.

Love,
Vera

WHO (NOT WHAT!) ARE THE ACADIANS? A sense of history and a sense of humor add much to one's enjoyment of genealogical searching.

{V}

Augusta, Georgia

Dear Bette,

Yes, I heard your area is having very cold weather. We are, too. They promised us an ice storm and some snow. I ran out to buy seed for the wild birds and my husband was quite upset that I didn't think to buy any "people" food at the same time!

As for your question, "What are Acadians?" My dear girl, they aren't a "what," they are a "who." This was the name given to the French who settled in the Maritime section of New France (to distinguish them from their countrymen who settled along the St. Lawrence River) in 1605, in a section which includes present-day Nova Scotia, New Brunswick, and Prince Edward Island of the Canadian Maritime Provinces, and which the French called "Acadie." French claims to the territory were based on Varrazano's voyage of 1524, but England claimed it from the Cabots' 1497-1498 voyages. The English captured it from the French in 1613 and in 1621 granted Acadie to Sir William Alexander, in the process discarding "Acadie" in favor of "New Scotland,"--"Nova Scotia."

In the years between 1605 and 1713, this area (and its names) were bandied back and forth between the British and the French, and only a treaty in 1713 finally made it a British colony. During all this time, the poor Acadians tried to stay out of the way of both armies, but nevertheless, they were mistreated because they weren't really trusted by either side. Then in 1755, England and France were at war again and the British colonial authorities, doubting the loyalty of the French Acadians, took their land away from them, sold or granted it to settlers who they knew were loyal, then ran them out of Nova Scotia. Running for their lives (either this, or be sent back to France), some 6,000 Acadians left in 1755, spreading out all over New England while some went farther west and others headed south; many present-day "Cajuns" of Louisiana are descended from the Acadians (A<u>cadi</u>ans = <u>Caj</u>uns, get it?). Later about 3,500 more of them went back to France. As the encyclopedia says, after 1763 "it was a story of a people, not a country." Some of the Acadians stayed in the Maritimes, and as an interesting footnote of history, by the mid-20th century, there were almost a quarter of a million of their descendants in the Canadian Maritime Provinces. As the exiles looked for a new place to settle, families weren't always able to stay together. Some were lucky enough to reunite with their loved ones years later, but others never saw their families again.

If someone knows he is of French descent, and has traced the family into upper parts of New England, then he should go one step further: check Nova Scotia's history and see if his ancestor could have been one of the unfortunate Acadians. But there, too, you need to study history. New Brunswick, Canada, was actually Nova Scotia until the late 1700s. In fact, Nova Scotia of that early period reached right down into what is now the state of Maine. Maine has the Acadia National Park on Mount Desert Island, about 50 miles southeast of Bangor. This park was once part of the French province of Acadie, so that gives you an idea of how vast an area what is now Nova Scotia used to be.

Honey, sometimes you get so interested in the history of an area or its people when you're researching that you forget what you went "there" looking for. Try it. Does that answer your question?? Write soon.

Love,
Vera

P.S.: My reference to the 1497-1498 Cabot voyages reminded me of a toast given at a Holy Cross Alumni midwinter dinner 75 years ago--thought it might give you a midwinter chuckle today. "And this is good old Boston, The home of the bean and the cod, Where the Lowells talk to the Cabots, And the Cabots talk only to God." Genealogy searches lead to all kinds of fun things, don't they?

FREEMAN'S OATH. Terms used in old records can cause confusion, but chasing down their meanings can lead you to fascinating chapters in history.

{v}

Dear Bette,

It was good to hear from you, and to hear that I've finally convinced you of the need to make your files as accurate as possible.

Your new question about your New England ancestors amused me--"What is a freeman?" For years I had the same idea that you have, that it means someone who had indentured himself for a period of years to the person who paid his passage money, and he was now free of that indenture. This won't be the only time you'll find that it takes a history lesson to clear up a problem. Briefly, very briefly, here's some background:

The Massachusetts Bay Company was an English association formed to trade in New England and in 1629 the company was given a royal charter by King Charles I to that effect. It was also given a huge grant of land in New England ("from sea to sea"!) and given power to govern within the grant's boundaries. The governor and his assistants and another group, the "freemen," were to share power, but the powers of each group were not clearly defined. Problems of representation, taxation, and religion soon erupted. In 1631, it was enacted that only members of the Puritan Church could become freeman; non-Puritans were denied the vote (sounds like history repeating itself from some of the European countries, doesn't it?).

Anyway, in order to be eligible to be elected a freeman, a man had to be a Puritan and he could not be an indentured servant. And, once elected, he had to take the Oath of a Freeman (the Oath is said to be the first work printed by the English in North America), which read as follows:

I, _____ , being by God's providence an inhabitant and
freeman within the jurisdiction of this Commonwealth, do fully acknow-
ledge myself to be subject to the government thereof, and therefore do
hereby swear by the great and dreadful name of the everlasting God that
I will be true and faithful to the same, and will accordingly yield
assistance and support thereunto, with my person and estate, as in
equity I am bound, and I will also truly endeavor to maintain and
preserve all the liberties and privileges thereof, submitting myself to
the wholesome laws and orders, made and established by the same. And
further, that I will not plot nor practice any evil against it, nor
consent to any, that shall do so, but will truly discover and reveal
the same to lawful authority now here established, for the speedy
preventing thereof. Moreover, I do solemnly bind myself in the sight
of God, that when I shall be called to give my voice, touching any
such matter of this state wherein freeman are to deal, I will give
my vote and suffrage, as I shall judge in mine own conscience may best
conduct and tend to the public weal of the body, without respect of
persons or favor of any man, so help me God in the Lord Jesus Christ.

Until the expiration of the first charter, in 1684, this Company--with its freemen--made the laws and governed completely all other settlers. And though it was an honor to be elected, you can see by this oath that the man practically pledged everything he had for that honor.

People were the same then as they are today, most honoring the oath they took, but some used it to their own advantage. Say that you didn't have water on your land, and your neighbor had a pond on his --you could go to the officials and say you heard your neighbor say seditious things about the government. His land was then confiscated and he was run out of the area. And then, as a good citizen, you had the chance of taking over his property, and no one questioned YOU, you were a freeman with the Company. Do go to your library one day and read up on the Massachusetts Bay Company, you'll find it fascinating!

Numerous settlers refused to become freemen and had another kind of oath to take, but I'll go into that some other time.

Love,
Vera

P.S.: I forgot to tell you that a List of Freemen of Massachusetts, 1630-1691, is available from the Genealogical Publishing Co. in Baltimore; it's a reprint from issues of The New England Historical and Genealogical Register in 1849.

{*v*}

Augusta, Georgia

Dear Bette,

I must admit that genealogical abbreviations are a big confusing, but PLEASE, stop using your imagination--<u>that</u> is not what "atba" means!!

When the early settlers arrived, they cleared land, built homes, and planted gardens, disregarding the fact that the land wasn't theirs to take. Naturally the Indians weren't going to sit back and let strangers take what was theirs, so they destroyed everything they could and killed those who resisted. Soon, leaders of these settlements realized that they needed to form a defense against these attacks. They went to each small town, making lists of all the men 16 to 60 years of age who knew which end of a gun to point at the enemy. These men were provided with arms and ammunition to protect the people in their area. Many of these lists still exist today, giving the names (often not to be found elsewhere) of early settlers. They're entitled "Able To Bear Arms," which genealogists have abbreviated to "atba."

I can't resist adding a little "color" to this lesson. By late 1643, most towns had formed a militia and had regular training sessions, BUT, the soldiers not only didn't get paid, they actually had to pay a certain amount into the company every three months for the privilege of being allowed to serve (wonder who thought of that one!). Among the many rules governing these companies was this one: "When a man from the company dies, the entire company must come together, with their arms, and inter his corpse as a soldier." This must have been the beginning of the modern-day military funeral.

Finding "bits of history" like this is almost as much fun as finding a new ancestor. Don't you find it interesting? (You'd better!)

Love,
Vera

"INTENTIONS" VERSUS MARRIAGES. The importance of proving an ancestor's marriage date and not just assuming that a marriage was solemnized because a bond was taken.

{V}

Augusta, Georgia

Dear Bette,

What do they mean in genealogy by "intentions of marriage?" Well, it's about the same thing as taking out a license these days. You have to be very careful of the lists of Intentions. Many a marriage that has been claimed on lineage charts never took place because people don't understand that "intentions" and "marriage" are two different things. Just like today, couples who applied for a license sometimes changed their minds and didn't marry.

While we're on this subject, you might as well learn about marriage bonds. In this case, the groom (and his bondsman) had to post bond, obligating himself to pay up if something from his past prohibited him from making the marriage contract. The bond became void when the marriage was solemnized. If the groom got cold feet at the last minute and backed out of the marriage, it was also void. The bond was issued in the county of the bride's residence. But remember, finding a bond does not a marriage make!

So you see that intentions of marriage, marriage bonds, and posting banns on the church door are all basically the same thing. The prospective groom is telling all the other guys, "She's already spoken for, keep your distance!! And besides, I can take care of her and a family."

We're supposed to have snow tomorrow and this little old Yankee can hardly wait--come have some fun with me.

Love,
Vera

Chapter 12

Cemeteries: A Genealogist's Last Resort??

Outdoor museums, they are. Places where you can reach out and touch history. And the stone "documents," you find there may bear the only death records you will ever find on elusive ancestors.

CEMETERIES ARE FINE PLACES FOR "ANCESTORIN'." Recipe: Take a nice sunny day, a picnic lunch, a county road map, and head for the country. There's <u>nothing</u> more fun for a genealogist than cemetery "ancestorin'."

{V}

Augusta, Georgia

Dear Bette,

It sounds like you and the others had fun going through the old section of the local cemetery. Don't you love the wording on some of the tombstones! But if you really want to have fun, find an old country cemetery that hasn't been used for years. Of course, you must research ahead of time to locate one of them, and a county highway map from your state's Department of Transportation office should show you were they are. Write them for a county map.

Don't make this type of trip without advance planning! The time of year is most important, because snakes are out in full force in the summertime and most country cemeteries are overgrown with grass and weeds then.

First, make a list of who you hope to find buried there. Try not to overlook anyone, as you may never get back there again. Remember to plan your trip for winter or spring, and to dress right (old clothes are the thing here). Take water, a hat, plenty of paper and pencils, a camera and several rolls of black and white film (it doesn't fade through the years), materials for rubbing the gravestones that won't photograph well (and the rubbings are nice to frame, too), a tape measure to record size of stone and grave (usually a 3-foot grave for a child, and a 6-foot grave for an adult), make sure you have a jack and an <u>inflated</u> spare tire (country roads may be rough), and your county map. This is just a basic list of needed things; as you make more forays into the country you will add to this list. The idea is to have everything you need to record everyone who belongs to you in that cemetery, so you don't have to return later.

Look for sinks, as many unmarked graves are usually found; grave measurements will tell you if the sink is a child's or an adult's grave. Be sure to record all graves, including the sinks. Take individual pictures of each one, and then an overall view of the entire cemetery. Draw a map showing the relation-ship of graves, one to the other--that may help you identify obscure family ties.

Copy everything on the stone exactly as it is and anything you're not sure of, enclose a note in brackets, like so: August 1<u>9</u>, and in brackets beside it, put [1<u>8</u>?]. Make notes of any markings that may give further clues, such as B.P.O.E. (says he was an Elk), or a stonecarver's name on the back of the stone. Don't miss anything!! By the way, the Augusta Genealogical Society has developed a great form for recording information on individual stones. They'll send you a sample if you send them an SASE; write AGS, PO Box 3743, Augusta, GA 30904.

Oh, dear! Forgot to tell you to pack a lunch! This is a must. Wherever you find this cemetery, there is another nearby, and there's no need to go back home without checking it out, too. So what if you have blisters, if you're hot and tired, and muddy and ache all over? You're having fun, aren't you? <u>Sure</u> you are!

Love,
Vera

"CEMETERYING" IS NOT GHOULISH. Some important reasons for searching cemeteries and tips for genealogists who look to cemeteries for information.

{V}

Augusta, Georgia

Dear Bette,

What do you mean searching cemeteries is ghoulish! I'll have you know that you can pick up a lot of clues on an ancestor in a cemetery!! You have the sexton records which cover opening and closing of the grave, and who owns which lot plus a "lot" more! Sometimes a fraternal emblem will be found, such as the Masons. Sometimes the maker of the tombstone has his name engraved on the back of the stone. All these things give you clues. In addition, records maintained at the national headquarters of churches or organizations, such as the DAR, can sometimes be used based on information learned from a tombstone. If you learn the name of the stonecutter, business records might show who purchased the stone.

And don't forget the things written on the stone--names and dates, etc. Of course, you have to know the "lingo." _Relict of_ means she (or he) was a widow or widower. . .consort of means the husband was still living (and, rarely, that wife was alive). . .wife of could mean she was wife or widow at death . . .in 89th year means the deceased has passed his 88th birthday, but not reached his 89th one. Some say "1808-1879". . .others say "died 25 April 1879, age 67 years, 3 months, 8 days" (this one will drive you crazy!).

To figure the birthdate from the above date is simple; you subtract the days, years, and months from it:

```
1879   4   25
  67   3    8
1812   1   17   (Born 17 Jan 1812)
```

Other subtractions aren't that easy, because you can't subtract a large number from a smaller number. Suppose you found this: "died 23 June 1835, age 42 years, 9 months, 29 days." Once written, it looks this way:

```
         17
1834   5   53
1835   6   23
  42   9   29
```

First, add 30 days to the righthand column, then take away one month. The middle column still can't be subtracted, so you must add 12 months to it (see?). Now, you must deduct that year from the year of death and you have this:

```
1834   17   53
  42    9   29
1792    8   24   (Born 24 Aug 1792)
```

This system isn't totally accurate, in that it doesn't take into consideration leap years or 31-day months. But it _is_ simple and will work out to the right year and month; the day is accurate within five days, so you could put in your records: "born 22 to 27 Aug 1792." And that's more than you knew before. Right??

Hope this has succeeded in showing you how much fun it is to search cemeteries. Besides, while you figuring out this complicated "birthdate thing" you don't have time to feel creepy.

Love,
Vera.

139

THE VA WILL SUPPLY HEADSTONES FOR DECEASED VETERANS. One's military research may lead to putting a marker on an ancestor's grave.

[V]

Augusta, Georgia

Dear Bette,

Let's talk about something serious for a change, okay? I want to tell you about grave markers for deceased veterans. Practically everyone has heard that they can get these markers, but few of us know how to go about it. As you can imagine, there are certain rules to follow--you can't just order one put on the grave and then send the bill to the government.

The Veterans Administration (VA for short) will furnish headstone or marker for a deceased veteran buried in any cemetery. An applicant may write to "Monument Service (42), Veterans Administration, 810 Vermont Ave., NW, Washington, DC 20420" and request VA Form 40-1330. Once the form is completed, you send it back to the same address along with a copy of the veteran's discharge, or with some official document pertaining to his military service. When the VA approves your application, the marker is shipped without charge to the applicant (or to someone you have previously designated). Remember that ALL COSTS TO INSTALL THE MARKER MUST BE PAID BY THE APPLICANT!!

There are several types of headstones and markers to choose from. One type of headstone or marker is furnished an applicant for the unmarked grave of a deceased veteran, and can be applied for by anyone having knowledge of the deceased. You must be sure the grave IS unmarked and that the family would prefer a government headstone. Another type is the Memorial Headstone or Marker which must be applied for by a relative recognized as next of kin. The Memorial Marker may be installed in any cemetery to commemorate any veteran whose remains have not been recovered or identified. This includes veterans of very early wars whose graves bear no marker and more recent veterans who were buried at sea, those whose bodies were donated to science, and those whose remains were cremated and the ashes scattered (provided no portion of the ashes was placed in a permanent resting place).

You have the choice of an upright marble headstone, or a flat marker made from marble or granite, bronze, or slate. Also, there are two special styles of up-right marble headstones available--one for those who served in the Union Forces in the Civil War or during the Spanish-American War, and another style for those who served in the Confederate Forces during the Civil War.

Mandatory items of inscription at government expense are: name, branch of service, and years of birth and death. If requested to do so, and at government expense, the VA will add grade, rank, war service, month and day of birth and death. Additional items will be inscribed at the applicant's expense, and must be approved by the VA. It is mandatory that memorial headstones or markers have the words "In Memory Of" inscribed on them.

Even though an applicant can get Form 40-1330 from the Washington, DC address above, don't overlook help closer to home. There is a VA Regional Office in each state and its toll-free phone number may be found in the phone book under "United States Government, Veterans Administration." These offices will be happy to assist you at any time. The staff at our office in Augusta has been most helpful to the citizens of the area in explaining the various types of benefits available to the next of kin of deceased veterans.

Eligibility for a marker is quite simple--any deceased veteran of wartime or peacetime, who was discharged under conditions other than dishonorable, is eligible.

This is a fine way to honor an ancestor whose military service you have documented.

Give my love to the family and write again soon.

Love,
Vera

"HAVE [CEMETERY] BAG, WILL TRAVEL." Since you never know when you're going to run across an old cemetery out in a field or forest, it's a good idea to be prepared for surveying the graves there!

{V}

Augusta, Georgia

Dear Bette,

While cleaning out the trunk of my car the other day, I found something that might interest you, since you and Chuck travel so much. A few years ago, I was complaining to a friend of mine, Carrie Adamson, about finding an old cemetery out in the country and not having a camera with me. Her first words were, "You don't have a cemetery bag in your trunk?" Well, I didn't, had never heard of one, BUT do have one now!! Carrie explained to me that she and Ray always keep one in their car, in case they run across an old cemetery and want to explore it. She also said that as soon as any of the supplies are used, they are replaced immediately. That way, the bag is always in traveling shape. It's a great idea and I'm sharing her "Have bag, will travel" idea with you. It goes like this:

Whenever you're out riding in the country, keep an eye out for a stand of cedars in a field, a fair sign of an old cemetery being there. In the spring, look for clumps of daffodils blooming, as they come up each year and may have decorated an old burying site.

Now, in the cemetery bag goes: A whistle fixed on a chain to wear around your neck, to summon help if needed; clippers for vines and brush; sponge and vinegar to clean the stones if necessary; chalk to outline an inscription for clarity, and a soft brush to dust off the chalk when finished; a sharp probe (such as a flower-support stick) to locate old possibly unmarked gravesites; a tape or yardstick for measuring gravestones and sections (and for making a map to show relationships of graves); scissors, camera, and clutter bag; Ziploc bag with washcloth; towel; something to kneel on (a large plastic bag filled with old newspapers in a good "kneeler"); felt-tip pen and paper; cemetery/individual gravesite survey forms for recording tombstone information; and a clip board to hold these forms while you are recording the data (it keeps papers from blowing away).To make tombstone rubbings, you need charcoal or a grease pencil (also called a china marker) and masking tape to secure rubbing paper (drafting paper, blank newsprint, butcher paper, etc.) to the stone.

The above list takes care of the cemetery, but what about YOU? For yourself, put in the bag a thermos of water (cemeterying is thirsty work!); calamine lotion; bug repellent; plastic bags and rubber bands for makeshift boots, to fit over any shoes you happen to be wearing (old fields are notorious for water and mud); and (this one is MY idea) a bag of popcorn (I always get hungry).

Two last things to remember. Always leave your purse locked up in the car trunk. It is "excess baggage" while you're in the cemetery having fun (and it IS fun!). Also, as you scout the cemetery, be sure to get all the information you need, you may never get back that way again (and even if you did get that way again, you might not be able to locate that cemetery). And, oh yes, always write down exactly what you see on the stones, never make a change to what you think it ought to be!

Since I know you so well, I also know the first question you're going to ask me after reading this letter--where did I get the cemetery/individual gravesite survey forms for recording the tombstone information? Right?? The answer is that I bought them from the Augusta Genealogical Soceity--they originated the forms and are they ever great!

Write soon and let me know how everyone is, and hug them all for me.

Love,
Vera

Chapter 13

"When Your Ox is in the Ditch"

Stone walls! There comes a time when no matter how or where you look, you can't find a solution to a knotty research problem. Here are a few ways to help you pull your ox out of the ditch!

143

A CLOSED MIND MEANS A CLOSED LINE. Although seemingly impossible things turn up in genealogical research sometimes, the seasoned searcher knows that almost anything is possible!

{v}

Augusta, Georgia

Dear Bette,

If you can write a letter like that, I'm not much of a teacher!! Thought you would have learned by now that in this business you "never say never." If you don't have documents to either prove or disprove a theory, how can you say, "THAT couldn't be MY ancestor."? You said that he was in the 1860 and 1870 censuses of Worcester County, Massachusetts, so the James Ferguson in Hampshire County, Massachusetts in 1866 <u>couldn't</u> be yours. So what if he <u>was</u> there at the time those censuses were taken--you don't know what he might have been up to in the intervening ten years. He might have taken a sea voyage, gone to visit the family in another state, his job might have taken him to another town for a few years, or, he might have done almost anything. The point is that you can't just say "he isn't mine" and forget him. He just might be the link you've been looking for IF YOU FOLLOW THROUGH ON YOUR INFORMATION.

If you think about it, you'll remember that we had this situation in our family before. Grandma's parents married in Connecticut in 1868, two years later their first daughter was born in Wisconsin, three years later the next child was born back in Connecticut. Now, if the early family researchers had said that the man in Wisconsin by the same name as our man, couldn't have been ours, why, poor Aunt Ada would never have gotten into the family.

To be more explicit: In family research, before you have actual proof one way or the other, you never make the statement, "It couldn't have been." When you've been in the business for awhile, and have tons of notes, you'll find that they are full of such phrases or questions as "might have been"..."could have been"..."maybe"..."was it?"..."could he have?"..."did he?"..."where did he go?"..."why did he go?"..."was there another wife (or husband)?"..."could she marry that young?"..."would she have a baby at that age?"--questions and more questions. But never, "It couldn't be."

From a modern point of view, you may not think a man would pack his wife and six small children into a wagon, travel several hundred miles from home, and resettle in some wilderness. But they did do it! And you'll never pick up their trail again by saying, "Nobody would be stupid enough to do that." You must keep your thoughts fluid, and keep your mind open to suggestion. After all, if you follow a man for several years, lose track of him for a few years, and then find him back at the old homeplace, it must tell you one thing (at least)--he had to be someplace during those "lost" years. So why not in Hampshire County? Have you a better idea? Follow through on it, you may get a nice surprise.

To be successful in family research, you must trace every man by that name living in that general area, until you can prove which one is yours.

This concludes the lesson for today (you don't have to act so happy!) but I will leave you with one thought: A CLOSED MIND MEANS A CLOSED LINE! Remember that.

Say hello to the family and write when you have time.

Love,
Vera

"KEEP AN OPEN MIND--AND LET IT WANDER." Follow that advice when you come up against a stone wall; research isn't cut and dried--you have to consider all the "possibles."

{v}

Augusta, Georgia

Dear Bette,

It was great to hear from you so soon after your last letter, but you seem to have a problem; you're not allowing your mind to work <u>for</u> you. Doing research is not "cut and dried." When problems come up, you must let your mind wander to all the possibles that might have taken place back then. You can't say, "they wouldn't have done that," or "they couldn't have lived there." You, of this time period, just couldn't judge your ancestors to that extent. Remember my theory of keeping an open mind. From the material you got off that death certificate it seems that your next step is a trip to the cemetery. This is the way to get a picture of a family, because a wife and some of their children are probably in the same plot. Tombstones are very informative, and you may find something on the wife if you make the effort to see the family plot. Let me show you a few things you might find.

John Smith's death record gives this: b. Oct 1748 at Newbury, MA, d. 3 Jan 1827 at Hartford, CT, buried in Franklyn Cemetery, and, parents were Joel Smith and Alice Jones. Space for a wife is blank, and that is your main interest. A trip to the cemetery gives you more information. There are tombstones for John, his wife Frances Green, and six children. Copy all the names and dates from each stone, then go home and make a simple fact sheet showing what you've learned. At the top begin with the data from the death record and go from there. The results looks something like this:

John Smith, b. Oct 1748 Newbury, MA, d. 3 Jan 1827 Hartford, CT, m before 1774
Frances Green, b. 1752, d. 1802, both buried Franklyn Cemetery, Hartford, CT
Known children, in order of birth are
   1. John   1774-1798 (d. age 24)
   2. Frances   1776-1781 (d. age 5)
   3. Joel   1778-1782 (d. age 4)
   4. Alice   1780-1840 (d. age 60)
   5. Luke   1782-1844 (d. age 62)
   6. Lucy Brown   1784-1862 (d. age 78)

Now look this over carefully and then make a list of the NEW things you learned. Ready?

You've learned that John's wife was Frances Green, that four children lived to be adults, that only one daughter married (Lucy Brown). You have the date that Frances died, so you can now check Hartford's death records and (let's hope!) find where she was born and her parentage. But, even before that, you do have a <u>possible</u> clue to her parents. Look at the names given the children. The first two were named after the parents, John and Frances. The next two were named after the parents of John. So, it is <u>possible</u> (and only a possibility at this point) that Luke and Lucy were named after the parents of Frances. Your chart must show that is conjecture and not fact (yet).

Your next step is the Hartford vital records. You must confirm these dates and you need to know if they married there, or if any of the children were born there. You see, at this point, you don't know if John and Frances met and married in Hartford, or in Newbury, or somewhere else entirely. Also, don't overlook the records of the cemetery itself; they show who bought the section, and would also show if the body (or bodies) had been brought from another place for burial.

Take this chart of a hypothetical family and apply the same concept to your problem. Will be interested in knowing if it helps. Won't ask you to write again because I'm sure you will; but take heart, you're learning quite fast. Say hello to everyone for me.

Love,
Vera

WHEN YOUR OX IS IN THE DITCH... When all else fails to bring an answer to your queries, dream up new ways to advertise your needs. Try posting notices in public places, newspaper ads, or radio spots! A zany idea may be just the ticket to get the ox moving!

{v}

Augusta, Georgia

Dear Bette,

All your recent letters talk about never getting answers to your queries you've sent out to various periodicals. That seems to be a problem for all of us, but sooner or later that query will be seen by someone who can help you. BUT--Honey, you are in a rut!! There are other ways to get your "wants" out into the public eye. Some of them are a little on the nutty side, while others are a logical way to go, but all are fun, and all get results. Let's try a few...(nutty ones first).

One lady wrote several years ago that every town she visited where her ancestors had lived, she "did the silliest thing." She had printed small cards listing the family of interest, her own name and address, and a promise to refund postage, and to share with anyone writing to her. Then she posted the cards on local laundromat walls! She said, "Boy, did I get results!"

Then I wrote to a radio station which served Washington County, Maine, asking if they could announce that I was trying to find descendants of one of the first settlers of Machias. A few weeks later an answer came from a lady in Maine--it turned out that her grandmother and my great-grandfather were brother and sister. Twenty years later I still write to, and share family data with, her daughter and grandson.

But the best, and most logical, way to get help with your "problem child" is so simple that most of us overlook it. One of our AGS members, Glover Bailie, Jr., told me how much luck he's had using the method. First, he locates a newspaper in the area where his ancestors were, then he writes out an advertisement asking for whatever information he's seeking. The next step is to write to the Editor asking rates for inserting an ad in their Personal Column (or however their newspaper does it). And don't forget to send an SASE!! Some of Glover's successes are:

He placed an ad in a paper in Houston, Texas, looking for the family of a man who had been killed in an accident off the coast. The mayor of a small town outside Houston read it, called the son of the deceased man and said, "Write this fellow."

Another time an ad was placed in a paper in Scranton, Pennsylvania. Glover was looking for some of his kin who had lived in a small town outside Scranton in the late 1800s; he even included the address from that time period. A short time later he received an envelope and an unsigned note saying that this family still lived at that address, and then listed the name of the family. Glover wrote to them, and later visited with them and had the pleasure of meeting relatives that he hadn't known existed before. They exchanged a lot of information that was beneficial to both branches of the family.

Glover said that his greatest pleasure came from being able to assist someone else to find his family and it couldn't have been done without newspaper advertising. A man in Colorado wrote to someone here in Augusta trying to find his brothers and sisters he'd been separated from at an early age. This man had been adopted, but he remembered the family name and that he'd had a twin brother. The letter made the rounds and ended up on Glover's desk--Glover placed an ad in the Augusta papers and waited. Six weeks later he placed the same ad again, and this time he had an answer from a lady who knew this family. The result was that the man in Colorado found his family, except for the twin brother who had died. Isn't that GREAT!!!

So why don't you try one, or all, of the above? Or let your mind run free and dream up ideas of your own (smart, logical, zany, outright crazy ideas are best!).

Love,
Vera

"WHICH JOHN?" How one pinpoints an ancestor when all that is known is his name, approximate birthdate, and the given name of his wife.

{V}

Augusta, Georgia

Dear Bette,

Sooner or later you'll run into the problem of finding your ancestor in a town, only to find that there are several men there by the same name and about the same age. There are probably a lot of ways to figure out who is who, but I'll show you one of them.

Suppose Grandpa said that your John Marshall came from St. George, Maine, and that he was born about 1760, and married a girl named Sarah, and that's all you have to work with. Basically, you need John's parents, and Sarah's maiden name. So you hightail it up to Maine and go through the vital records looking for two things: a John born about 1760, and a John who married a Sarah. Your "find" should look something like this:

Births:
       John, son of William and Sarah Marshall, b. 3 Nov 1759
       John, son of John and Elizabeth Marhsall, b. 13 Oct 1760
       John, son of Jacob and Anne Marshall, b. 10 Dec 1760
       John, son of Benjamin and Joan Marshall, b. 1 Jan 1761

Deaths:
       John d. Feb 1832   John d. April 1837
       John d. Oct 1842   John d. 24 Dec 1760, age 2 weeks

Marriages:
       John m. Sarah White Oct 1780
       John m. Sarah Wilson Aug 1782
       John m. Sarah Clark Jun 1783

Jacob's son was the one who was two weeks old on 24 Dec 1760--that eliminates one John. Where to go from there, as you're left with three in each category? Ah, yes, Grandpa said something else-- that your John served in the Revolutionary War. Now you need to get National Archives Form 80 (rev. 5/91) to request his service record, fill in the data asked for and send it off to Washington, DC--then you wait.

When his military and pension records arrive you're disappointed. All they tell you is that he enlisted at St. George in 1776, the officers he served under, that his wife was Sarah, and that he still had two minor children at home. But all is not lost--the Archives also included the widow's application for her deceased husband's pension, and it's a gold mine of information. The items of most interest to you are: Sarah is 87 years old (b. ca. 1766), that she and John married in June, 1783, and that he died on his 82nd birthday, 13 Oct 1842.

From the vital records above you can see that only one John fits this data and you have in your hands exactly what you were searching for. Your new data on John looks like this:

      John, b. 13 Oct 1760, son of John and Elizabeth Marshall,
      m. June 1783 Sarah Clark who was b. ca.1766. John d. 13
      Oct 1842, aged 82.

Using this method, you're not trying to prove which one is yours, but to prove which ones COULD NOT BE YOURS (then you have to take what's left, poor you).

Gee, this is fun (isn't it???)!!

                Love,
                Vera

"ASSUMING" IS A NO-NO! After years of cautioning others not to <u>assume</u> anything during their genealogical searching, Vera (like Homer) momentarily nodded, and fell into the trap herself.

{V}

Augusta, Georgia

Dear Bette,

Your letter arrived questioning my choice of parents and wife for John Marshall of St. George, Maine in my last letter to you. Wondering where I'd "gone wrong" in convincing you the solution was correct, out came my carbon of the letter. After carefully going over it, I decided, dear cousin, that you were nuts; it was the <u>only</u> solution! But I couldn't get it out of my mind (nag, nag, nag!!), and got the letter out again. I finally saw your point (also remembered that there are no nuts in <u>our</u> family).

I ASSUMED that you knew that all available military, pension, and bounty land records would be requested from the National Archives for <u>any</u> and <u>all</u> John Marshalls from Lincoln County, Maine. It's standard procedure in a case like this. And you're right--all three men did serve, did get pensions, and one got bounty land. Actually, comparing the three pension applications was what helped in the elimination process. One John stated that he couldn't "labor because of being wounded in battle, and I have a home to care for, my wife, and my only child who is retarded." No line of descent here?? The second John said he didn't have a record of his birth but "it was in 1759 soon after Halloween," and that "I and my wife are old and feeble and have no one to care for us in our old age, never having had any children." No line of descent here, either!! That left John who married Sarah Clark, and baptismal records showed they had a son, Augustus (not a very common name). The cemetery plot holds the graves of John and Sarah, their son, Augustus, and his wife, Agnes Freeman.

I ASSUMED that you knew that this Marshall line was direct male descent from 1635 to the present.

I ASSUMED that you knew I'd <u>documented</u> the line as each generation was discovered.

I ASSUMED that you knew Charles Marshall's death record said his parents were Augustus Marshall and Agnes Freeman, both of St. George, Maine.

And finally, I ASSUMED that, knowing me, you'd know that <u>all</u> available source records were searched to find which John had a son named Augustus.

So! My solution was right! But YOU were right, too, to criticize my presentation of this line, and the solution I arrived at. Do you see why? Read both letters carefully. It's because, having personally done the research, and being familiar with all the facts pertaining to the final solution, I ASSUMED that you also would know everything without my going into detail!

This is a mistake made by most people in their lifetimes--expecting the ones we talk to to have as much knowledge on <u>our</u> subject as we do. But this kind of thinking has no place in genealogical research. I've told you many times: never assume anything, always prove for yourself, and keep an open mind. Seems like I should take my own advice, doesn't it??

Hope this clears up the problem for <u>you</u>, and <u>I'll</u> try not to do any more "assuming."

Love,
Vera

ON THE FINE ART OF "LISTENING." There's an art to asking the right questions; there's an art to <u>listening</u> to the answer!

{**v**}

Augusta, Georgia

Dear Bette,

I had a letter from Joan yesterday and knew before opening it that she was upset about something (you could see the smoke coming out from under the sealed edge!!). We both know how knowledgeable she is on research, and always willing to share with anyone who asks. She knows what is available in her state, what time period the records cover, the type of records, and all the early settlers mentioned in them. In other words, if you've asked for help, then you should certainly <u>listen</u> to the answers! Right??

Joan said she spent four hours with this lady who had come seeking her help on a "problem" family. She told her where most of them were buried, tax records in six towns for this surname, eight townships where land records existed on them prior to 1800, and marriage and birth records available for these areas. She gave the precise sources (archives, library, etc.) where the woman could find all this data. Told her of several descendants still living in the area, including some addresses. Also mentioned the military records at the Adjutant General's Office, and the city directories at local libraries for the time periods the woman needed. (Don't we wish we'd had a fairy godmother like that when we started out!!!) By now, Joan was feeling very happy that she had been able to give this lady so many leads. BUT. . .

Not once in the four hours did the lady take notes or ask questions!!! Afterwards, she asked if Joan "did paid research," had anyone "already done these families," were there any places she could go where she'd find that this work had already been searched out and proved (a bunch of dumb questions!!).

Now Joan was disgusted! She realized this person not only didn't want the fun of researching the family for herself, but that she <u>had not listened</u> to a single thing she'd been told. What a waste of time!!! No wonder smoke was coming out of that envelope! I'm surprised the paper wasn't scorched, too. There are many people like this lady--they are thinking so much about what <u>they</u> are going to say when you stop talking, that they don't hear a word you've said. Or, maybe they think that what you're telling them isn't important <u>until</u> you get to the part they've been waiting for--that someone else has already done all the work for them. Don't they know how much fun they are missing out on?

I wrote Joan that she shouldn't get so angry, that she should feel sorry for the lady. There is nothing more satisfying to a family researcher than to find an ancestor's name in the records after spending hours (going cross-eyed) looking for him. And this lady, and others like her, will never know this feeling.

Grandma used to say, "If you don't know something then ask someone who does know." Vera now adds to that with, "If you ask someone who knows, then LISTEN!"

That's all the nagging for today. Love to the family and write when you can.

Love,
Vera

DON'T ABUSE ONE'S TRUST! When a researcher shares his or her material with you, it is done so as an act of trust. Changing <u>anything</u> in that material is an abuse of that trust.

{V}

Augusta, Georgia

Dear Bette,

Through the years, we've talked about "a little of everything," including the use of courtesy and good manners in dealing with other researchers. We all know that <u>nice</u> letters to the holder of records we need almost always bring results, whereas a demanding letter very seldom gets answered. So, today we're discussing courtesy of another kind--how we should handle records belonging to others who have been kind enough to share them with us (VERY important!!).

All serious researchers take great care to get the documentation to prove their work is factual. This involves the spending of huge amounts of time and money--I, myself, have certified documents that have altogether cost several hundred dollars. And that's just for documents alone. Add to that the thousands of miles you've traveled, the professional genealogists you've hired, the photocopies made of court and other records, the hundreds of hours spent going through musty old records and <u>trying</u> (!!) to decipher handwriting of a century or longer ago, etc. Then there are the hundreds of letters you've written through the years to anybody and everybody you thought may have the data you needed to fill in another empty limb on your family tree (it's a well-known fact that family researchers have kept the postal service solvent for years). Many of us have spent 30 or 40 years researching our various family lines and our records deserve to be treated with care and courtesy!!!! SO. . .

When others are willing to share their years of research with you, DON'T ABUSE THEIR TRUST!!! <u>Never</u>, <u>ever</u> change a single item on their charts, documents, manuscripts, or anything else they may send to you!! Not dates, states, counties, or towns, and above all, <u>never</u> alter names on their work!! And, very definitely, <u>never</u> circulate among other researchers any chart compiled by someone else that <u>you</u> have altered and left the compiler's name on! This is a betrayal of their trust, their years of research, their documentation on their lines. Make sure that you are never guilty of such an unprofessional thing as altering the lifetime work belonging to another researcher.

One other thought--if you have documentation that <u>proves</u> there's an error in the work of others, show them the courtesy of personal contact. Send them a copy of the record you've found, along with a cover letter explaining why you believe their records to be wrong. Then they can decide if this really is an error in their direct line, or is another person with the same name (a cousin or uncle, etc.). So remember-- it is <u>not</u> your right to change another person's records. The only "right" you have is to notify them of a possible error in his/her work.

That's it for tonight (aren't you glad?). Write again soon, and hug the kids for me.

Love,
Vera

FIVE DIFFERENT BIRTH YEARS FOR ONE ANCESTOR? Not to worry! Just keep a list of them and any other conflicting information until you can verify and document the correct one.

{V}

Augusta, Georgia

Dear Bette,

Your last letter confused me quite a bit--how can you be so <u>sure</u> that you have the right birth date? From what you said in your letter, his gravestone gave one date, and the census another date. If you don't have a death or birth certificate to verify it one way or the other, you just <u>can't</u> pick one source and say "that's right." When doing family research you come across this problem often. My grandmother was called "Maggie," and I was told that she was Margaret Florence Munson; when her birth record was found, it showed she was actually named <u>Florence Margaret</u> Munson. A small error, but enough to send you after a record that's in another name entirely.

I have a friend here in Augusta who has a problem along this line, too. Barbara was told by a relative that her great-grandfather was James Ebenezer Rhoades, Jr., and he was buried in a private cemetery in Edgefield County, South Carolina (probably Graniteville), and that his wife was Saran Ann Rearden, who died in Abbeville, South Carolina, but was buried here in Augusta, Georgia. Simple, huh?? Not on your life!!! Knowing that her grandfather was born 1863 in Graniteville, she read the 1870 census, and found her first problem: James Ebenezer was really James W. The second problem came when she discovered that, at the time he would have died, Graniteville was in Aiken County, not Edgefield County. These problems were nothing compared to what she ran into with James' wife!

Since Sarah was buried in Augusta, Barbara went to the Board of Health and got her death record. Here we go again!!--Sarah really died in Calhoun Falls, South Carolina, in the <u>county</u> of Abbeville, not the town! And although she was shown as "<u>nee</u> Rearden," her father was listed as John <u>Redden</u>. The death certificate went on to state that she was b. 5 Mar 1841, d. 12 Dec 1925 at age 86 years, 9 months, 7 days (do you see this error?). Which is correct-the birth date given, or her age at death? Because when you subtract her age at death from her death date you get a birth date of 5 Mar 1839!! (Are you still there?) Locating the local cemetery where Sarah is buried, Barbara hightails it up there. She's going to clear this up once and for all--she's going to take pictures. Did she get a shock! The tombstone says: b. 5 Aug (what happened to March?) <u>1844</u>, d. 11 Dec 1925--a completely different set of dates from what was on the death certificate. The 1870 census said b. 1838 (age 32), and the 1880 census said b. 1840 (age 40).

When she compared these four supposedly reliable sources, she had this:
a) 1870 census: b. 1838
b) 1880 census: b. 1840
c) Tombstone: b. 5 Aug 1844
d) Death certificate: b 5 Mar 1841 and, using <u>age at death</u>, 5 Mar 1839

There are two different birth months and five different birth years, covering a span of six years. And Barbara <u>still</u> doesn't know which is correct!

My advice to her was that when you gather conflicting data like these facts on one person, LIST EACH EVENT, EACH DATE, AND EACH SOURCE IN YOUR RECORDS. Do not make any decision on which date is correct unless, or until, you can back it up with documentation! Take my word for it, whichever date you choose, it will be the wrong one.

Hope everyone is well there, and tell me--when is the new grandchild due? Have found a few more gray hairs since the news came. Oh, well, it comes to us all. Write soon.

Love,

Tina

WHY LOOK FOR AN ANCESTOR'S MEDICAL RECORD? Since we inherit the genes that make us what we are, we should look for our ancestors' medical records and add the information to our family charts.

{V}

Augusta, Georgia

Dear Bette,

Someone once said that, "all of your ancestors went into the making of you." This IS true and this letter will attempt to explain the importance of collecting medical records on your ancestors, as well as on your immediate family. All of us have a little knowledge about "inheriting" certain characteristics, and some know they come from the genes we got from our parents. And, of course, we're all familiar with the "Mean Gene." That is the one that gives curly hair to boys, while we girls get the straight hair. But few have given it deeper thought.

My interest in this subject began with a letter from the Center for Human Genetics in Bar Harbor, Maine. It was addressed to "Dear Genealogist," and signed by a Dr. Thomas H. Roderick, Ph.D., Geneticist, Certified Genealogist. He told about a family referred to the Center because of severe color blindness and very poor vision. The family was worried about the severity of this problem, and its effect on their children. Dr. Roderick collected a history of the family and then made arrangements for a Boston physician to run special tests. He emphasized that the diagnosis could not have been made with any accuracy without the detailed history of this disorder in this family. The physician in Boston had another patient with the same problem in Plymouth County, Massachusetts, and Dr. Roderick arranged to visit her. The first thing he discovered was that her family originally came from a town in Maine about 50 miles from the first family. Dr. Roderick's now searching the records in both states, trying to confirm that these two families were related "back then."

Later, another patient with this same eye problem was referred to him, and research into this man's family turned up the fact that he was a half-first cousin of the woman in Plymouth County. Dr. Roderick went on to say that because of the family histories he collected, the Center was able to tell the families the name of the disease, and the risk and severity to future descendants. This very rare genetic disorder is blue cone monochromatism and is characterized by very poor vision and total lack of color perception.

Another eye disorder of importance to many people, because it is common, is Retinitis Pigmentosa (RP). It's a progressive hereditary disorder characterized by night blindness and it often leads to blindness. The Center for Human Genetics now has a Retinitis Pigmentosa (Pronounce it?--not me!) Project. Its purpose is to locate and identify all Maine families with this disorder, and then to arrange diagnostic tests and counseling for the families. This doesn't mean just people living there now--it means anyone with Maine ancestry!

My curiosity aroused, I called the Center and talked to Dr. Roderick's staff and they graciously answered my question. A trip to the library answered the rest. Did you know that there are many independent groups around the country, formed by doctors dedicated to exploring genetic disorders and their causes, and hopefully, finding a cure? I say they are dedicated because these doctors DONATE (that means free) their time, their knowledge, and their own money--that's dedication in its highest form! Being independent organizations, they aren't attached to, or funded by, a large hospital, so they must rely on contributions from their patients and others interested in their work. These research centers have found over 2,000 disorders that are genetically inherited: sickle cell anemia, Huntington disease, some forms of diabetes, various heart problems, and hemophilia, to name just a few.

By now you're getting ready to ask, "What has all this to do with genealogical research?" Well, if your doctor is told about certain disorders that "run" in your family he will be more alert to any symptoms

YOU may have in that same direction. This will enable him to pinpoint the problem quicker, treat it sooner, and possibly save your life or that of one of your family.

Your "Lesson" for today is this: Make a list of your family as far back as you can, then beside each name write the cause of death and any other medical diseases they had when alive. Now compare them with each other. I'll bet you find the same thing I did!! Generation after generation--the same diseases and the same causes of death. Fascinating thought, isn't it, that you could predict ahead of time, and possibly prevent, the medical problems of your descendants.

So, from now on while you're collecting all those names, dates, and places of your ancestors be sure to get their medical histories--and don't forget to add that data to your charts.

Love,

Vera

WOULD YOU LIKE TO BECOME A "DAUGHTER?" (A "DAR," THAT IS.) Joining the DAR is the goal of many a genealogist. The rules are simple, but precise. Here they are, step by step.

{V}   Augusta, Georgia

Dear Bette,

      You must be very pleased with yourself to have finally found enough proof to be able to join the Daughters of the American Revolution, as I know you've dreamed of that for years. Now you want to know <u>how</u> to become a member, right?? The first thing to know is that membership in most patriotic organizations is by invitation only. So that means that you must find a member of the local chapter, meet with her, and discuss your desire to join her chapter with her. If you seem sincere to her, she can become your sponsor, and see to it that you meet other members.

      The rules for a prospective DAR member are set by the National Society and are quite simple. The applicant must be age 18 or over and must be able to prove direct-line descent from the ancestor she has chosen to join on; she must be known to at least two members in good standing with the chapter (they will become her endorsers); and the entire chapter must be allowed to vote on her acceptability. Usually, your sponsor will take you to one meeting as her guest for the purpose of giving all members a chance to meet and talk with you. Then she sends a letter to the Chapter Registrar sponsoring you as a prospective member, and names your two endorsers. The Registrar places the matter before the Executive Board and they vote on it. Once their decision is made, the Registrar takes over--at the next meeting she will read your name to the entire chapter and tell them something about you.

      At the next meeting, she does the same thing and then passes out ballots for the members to vote for, or against, you. Once you've been accepted, the Registrar sends out a welcoming letter to you, accompanied by a set of application papers, a work sheet, and instructions on how to complete these papers. Just to make things easier for you, for the Registrar, and for the genealogist at the National Society, don't do <u>anything</u> before reading that instruction sheet!! Each society has its own rules on how to fill out application papers and nothing else is acceptable to them, so the instructions that are sent to you are of the utmost importance.

      And now your fun begins! Take out the work sheet and with <u>pencil</u> fill in all the names, dates, and places that you can. Note that the papers are set up by generation--yours first, then parents, then grandparents, and so on, back to the ancestor you've chosen. Only enter in data that you can prove. You <u>must</u> document each statement made by you for every generation. Nothing else is acceptable. In the space provided, list the documentation for each generation; that way, you'll know what you already have, and what you will need to find. Mark each copy with the number of the generation it applies to (your birth and marriage records would be marked #1), then when you are finished with the typing of the set of application papers, it will be a simple matter to line up your proof for each generation, as required. It also assists the genealogist in checking your papers. (One important thing: never send original documents with your papers to the Registrar. Instead, make photocopies and keep the originals in your file for later use.)

      Although it's the responsibility of the applicant to research and complete her own papers, she is not without help from within the chapter. Once she's reached a deadend, a call to her sponsor, the Registrar, or the Lineage Research Chairman will bring help to her. They will not do the actual research, but they will advise on other sources and other documents that may prove a marriage when a certificate can't be found. Their help is invaluable, so avail yourself of it if it becomes necessary--they sometimes know of odd sources where information can be found that would never occur to many people. Lots of luck, and

Love,
Vera

"BARK & PURR." For all families who feel their pets _are_ a part of the family, here's an idea to give them their own chapter in the family saga!

{V}

Augusta, Georgia

Dear Bette,

As you know, many genealogists are now using the computer to record their family histories on disks. This is great because it also lets you share, with less trouble, all of your data with those who write to you. Have you mastered your computer yet? Have you purchased a genealogy program? Most programs I've seen advertised make charts for you to fill in with your info, alphabetically list "oodles" of your ancestors, and much more, but basically it's the same thing you've been doing with pre-printed forms.

Now I'm going to tell you about a new kind of computer program marketed by a firm in Texas--I haven't used it, but it sounds like great fun. I learned about it from one of our AGS members, Robert Miller of Kingsport, Tennessee. He said his family gave it to him as a Christmas present and he has thoroughly enjoyed using it.

Dr. Miller said that after answering all the questions asked for each chapter you can print out an entire "book" of history on each individual in the family. He also said it comes complete with a user's manual so detailed that even a novice computer-user can understand (and that sure means _me_!).

The program is called "Memories" and has over 1,200 questions to "interview" you, or others in the family, on events in your life. You don't have to respond to _all_ questions; for instance, one chapter is called "The Birds & the Bees," and other is called "Mischief" (things you got into when young). My favorite one is called "Bark & Purr" (all the pets the family owned). One thing for sure, whoever dreamed up the titles certainly had a sense of humor.

This program isn't rigidly constructed--you can add your own chapters or topics, or change the name of existing ones, or you can rearrange the order of those listed. Requirements to use the program are: IBM personal computer or compatibles with a minimum of 256K memory and two disk drives. If you're interested in obtaining this program, you may call this toll-free number: 1-800-637-9949.

Hon, if I ever learn to use the computer my brother, Dick, sent to me, I promise you "Memories" will be the first on my list of "wants." It sounds like fun to use and you know how I like to have fun!!

Well, dear, must close and finish lunch. My love to the family and write soon.

Love,
Vera

79. Nathan Boftick
    son of Wm Bostick   Burk
80. Sarah Drake, Widow   Jefferson
81. Thos Carpenter   Do
82. Josiah Carpenter   Do
83. Richd Chote   Do
84. John Coleman   Do
85. Sampson Chance   Do
86. Peter Chastain
    For Wm Howle

Vollentine Hatcher

Matthew Dorton

Epilogue

And after all that, "Why Genealogy?"

Because it's fun, that's why!

157

IT'S JUST PLAIN GOOD FUN, THAT'S WHAT GENEALOGY IS! The grand old man of genealogy, Donald Lines Jacobus, once said that genealogy is like working out a chess problem, but more exhilarating, for the pawns in this game were once living human beings. And look at all the fringe benefits in <u>this</u> game!

{v}

Augusta, Georgia

Dear Bette,

So, one of your friends wants to know why you're doing family research and you didn't have an explanation good enough to satisfy her? Of course you do! Just think about it, then write down all the reasons you've stayed hooked on it for eight years. Shall I start you off?

First, you have all the stuffy reasons that you began this research for--like WHO your ancestors were. We all begin by thinking <u>our</u> ancestors were a cut above everyone else's (hence the capitalization of WHO above). By the time we've dug up several average, everyday type of ancestors, we don't care <u>who</u> anymore. We've gotten so involved in how they lived, what their beliefs were, how they moved all over the country, and whether they were doctors, lawyers, farmers, or devilish rascals, that we are well and truly on the way to being a "genealogy nut." We aren't satisfied until we've collected everything available on their parents, siblings, children, and wife or wives. In other words, we nose into every aspect of their lives (fun, huh?).

Then you have the medical reasons. As you collect documents you also collect "causes of death" and that's important to your family and your descendants. Many diseases today have been proved to be inherited, and if your doctor is alerted to the diseases that "run" in your family, that may help him to avert some of them.

And what about filling in the spaces in your bride's book or your first baby's book? If you don't know about the great-grandparents, how can you fill in these books? A friend of mine had the wrong great-grandmother listed in her bride's book for years--and the information was given by the bride's mother! So another reason to trace your ancestry is to build a "family" for your descendants--a factual family.

One of the best reasons for doing family research is all the lovely, giving people that you meet through the years. They share their information and family anecdotes with you, and all they ask in return is for you to share with them whatever you have. Most of us have built up a large circle of friends during our research years and carry on correspondence with them long after the original reason for writing is gone. We learn about their children and grandchildren, what they grow in their gardens and preserve for use during the winter, the hobbies they have, and if they've lost a loved one, we grieve with them. In other words, we have made lifetime friends. What other hobby can give you the pleasure of such sharing!

Hon, I've saved the very, very best reason for last. Why you're doing family research is because it's just plain, darn good FUN!!! Am I right or am I right?!

Give my love to the family and write again soon.

Love,
Vera

Subject Index